.95
ned

Porcher's Creek

North

Highway 17

Dirt
Road

Porcher's Bluff

Porcher's Creek

to Copahee & Hamlin Sounds

C. T. Leland

Porcher's Creek

Lives between the Tides

John Leland

University of South Carolina Press

© 2002 University of South Carolina

Published in Columbia, South Carolina, by the
University of South Carolina Press

Manufactured in the United States of America

06 05 04 03 02   5 4 3 2 1

Library of Congress Cataloging-in-Publication Data

Leland, John, 1950–
    Porcher's creek : lives between the tides / John Leland.
        p. cm.
    ISBN 1-57003-457-5 (cloth : alk. paper)
    1. Salt marshes—South Carolina. 2. Fishing—South Carolina—Anecdotes.
    3. Nature—Effect of human beings on—South Carolina. 4. Leland, John,
    1950– I. Title.
    QH105.S6 L45 2002
    577.69'09757'91—dc21   2001007089

For Sarah, with love

Contents

Acknowledgments

I wish to thank the Virginia Military Institute for its generous support of this project. I especially thank Janet Holly and Elizabeth Hostetter of Preston Library for their assistance. I would like to thank Billy Baldwin for his expert advice concerning the manuscript. I thank USC Press, Ray Soulard, and Scott Burgess for the meticulous job they did of editing the manuscript. My sister Caroline provided the frontispiece. My sisters Elizabeth and Cheves and my brother Timothy and his wife Cindy all generously helped in reading the manuscript. My wife, Sarah Clayton, supported me throughout the writing of this book; her enthusiasm and advice were invaluable. I thank my father for the gift of the creek.

Introduction

A man, yet by these tears a little boy again,
Throwing myself on the sand, confronting the waves,
I, chanter of pains and joys, uniter of here and hereafter,
Taking all hints to use them, but swiftly leaping beyond them,
A reminiscence sing.

Walt Whitman

Summer, and I'm swimming in the creek again. At high tide, Porcher's Creek merges with Copahee Sound in a sheet of water four miles wide; six hours later at low tide, the sound becomes a maze of oyster-studded islands as pathless as any swamp. Before low tide is when I swim, floating down to Copahee in my inner tube with the outgoing water. Copahee's oyster islands, or banks as they are called, emerge grey-green and heavy from the water like the backs of a dozing school of armor-plated leviathans. Each bank is home to thousands of algae-dripping oysters, each oyster stuck to the other in a nightmare jumble of razor-sharp edges waiting to slice the careless arm or leg brushing against them. From the perforated shells of many oysters, sponges sprout red, orange, and white fingers that grope skyward like the fingers of corpses. The air is thick with salt, and over everything the mud has spread its cloying perfume.

I float back on the rising tide, letting it carry me landward through the maze of disappearing oyster banks to the equally confusing tangle of salt creeks, their miles of impenetrable water alive with ripples, gurgles and plops of unseen life-forms swimming beneath my inner tube. Channeled between oysters and mud surmounted by a green wall of marsh grass too high to see over, twisting and turning at random, the creek becomes two, three, five equally plausible routes, each beckoning me round the next voluptuous curve, and then the next, leading me inevitably into an ever-narrowing corridor of green that closes in until it hangs heavily over my lost head and, inner tube mired, I heave myself upright. Ploosh, the ground dissolves and I sink into primordial soup while round me rises the anaerobic stench of hydrogen sulfide. I'm alone, stuck waist deep in pluff mud, miles from land, and the tide is rising.

God, it's great to be home again.

Time passes and the tide continues to rise, floating me up and through the marsh grass itself, one of the least-touched wildernesses left in the United States. Here is a prairie stretching from New England to Texas, never plowed, never inhabited, seldom visited. The little bit I know runs from Charleston Harbor fourteen miles south of Porcher's to the Santee River twenty miles north. Two or three miles wide where I am now, the marsh is a mix of prairie, creek, and open water. Eastward the barrier islands—Sullivan's, the Isle of Palms, Dewee's, Caper's, Bull—guard it from the Atlantic's wrath; westward, the mainland runs in a solid line breached here and there by larger creeks— Porcher's, Awendaw, Jeremy. I passed my youth in these marshes, as did my father, and his father, and all my forefathers for as long as Lelands have lived on this coast, for over two hundred years. I can still float here in the six-foot-high marsh grass, where the land is too muddy to build on, and the water too salty to drink, but inland I cannot go.

Where Porcher's pierces the mainland, where once I fished and swam and hunted arrowheads, strangers dwell. My nursery is their backyard, my kindergarten their golf course, where they chase balls beside a creek they cannot name. Their docks so choke the creek that neither boat nor dolphin nor I dare ascend to traditional fishing holes. Cement slabs for half-a-million dollar houses cover four-thousand-year old Indian relics, and marauding bulldozers fill slave-dug ditches and levees. Hate-fences and guard-gates surround "exclusive" developments. No one but the inhabitants may enter "their" marsh, and they prefer the marsh at arm's length, through a window. They have posted Porcher's with signs:

DANGER
DO NOT ENTER
ALLIGATORS, POISONOUS
SNAKES AND SPIDERS.

My father knew Porcher's for over eighty years, and he will die here. The creek and my father run, inextricably intertwined, through my life and memories. I am what I am, for better or worse, thanks to my father and the creek he taught me to love. I had hoped to pass on to my son the creek my father's father had passed on to his son, but I cannot. I had hoped to die beside Porcher's, but I will not, because the way of life Porcher's banks nourished for over five thousand years has vanished.

The creek's inhabitants, human and other, once lived by Porcher's rhythms and seasons. Her tides commanded when we rose and slept, her seasons what we ate. The very land we lived on was built from her oyster shells, and our public rituals—oyster and fish roasts, crab and shrimp boils—depended on Porcher's. We therefore knew and liked Porcher's better than many people we met.

Porcher's is no more. There is a creek where she once flowed, and I walk it at low tide, swim its marshes at high tide. I still take oyster and clam, fish, crab, and shrimp from it, but Porcher's is gone, eviscerated, violated. Where once salt air and herons woke us, automobiles and slamming doors announce the new day. What once were soft and curving banks are lined and wrinkled now by the wake of power boats; cans and bottles and cups litter the fringing marshes, which shine with the ooze of oil; the cries of golfers fill air that used to ring with marsh hen, egret and whippoorwill.

Come with me while I take a farewell float down my creek and through my life. My generation may well be the last to know the vestiges of a life older than the pyramids, a way of life irrelevant to those who inherit our home. These newcomers, as secure today as we were yesterday, will, in the creek's own good time, be driven out. The sea rises, drowning five-thousand-year old Indian villages; hurricanes erase without a trace antebellum houses. People more knowledgeable than we promise an ever more quickly rising sea, ever more violent hurricanes. Look, even now, the tide laps higher at the land's edge. Come on, let's go while there is yet a creek to visit.

Porcher's Creek

1

Marsh

As a boy, I would take our bateau out exploring. Dependent upon tide and wind and oar, I learned early to know when the tide would turn, when I could float down or up creek without effort, letting the creek's ebb and flood work for me. Stuck in a lowland with no falling water, settlers harnessed the tides, as had the Indians before them. Charleston boasted mills powered by the tide, whose wheels threshed and ground rice grown in fields flooded by tides; early churches met at hours determined by the tides, for the convenience of far-flung settlers.

I knew none of this, only that following the current made exploring easier. Armed with water bottle and sandwich, carrying like Ulysses my oars upon my back, I'd hie me to the water's edge, right our bateau, turned over to protect it from weather, ship oars and food and water and push myself out onto the main.

Columbus knew no greater thrill than I did, a ten-year-old discovering new creeks and branches and islands and mainland hideaways. Corrupted by reading, I claimed new worlds for Leland, planting a crude cross or carving my initials into a convenient tree. I resolved to make my living as an explorer and said so in school when we were all asked what we planned to do upon growing up. My unthinking teacher opined to general laughter that there were no new worlds to explore. My adult life has been a limited one in part because, good pupil that I was, I listened to him. Had I not, perhaps I'd now be floating down the headwaters of the Amazon. As it is, I navigate an inner Amazon whose length and depth and breadth I cannot guess.

In my youth I had not yet listened to my betters, and so I passed a Huckleberry Finn sort of life. Though no Mississippi, Porcher's Creek had commerce of a sort and characters enough. Henry Manigault collected oysters as a second income, poaching them from Copahee Sound. Manigault figured he had proprietary rights to everything Copahee produced; it was his water, even if Phil Porcher thought he owned the oyster banks. Porcher didn't mind; there were plenty of oysters for both him and Manigault, who would float out from the Beehive Landing two miles north of Porcher's Creek. Winters I could find him in the lower reaches of the creek, his beaten bateau awash with oysters, conchs, clams, and whatever wonders the creek had offered that day. Manigault was famous for his stutter, his "h-h-how y-y-you do-do-doing t-t-today" taking him a painful minute to get out. The creek, however, soothed his stutter, washing it smooth with its sibilant whisperings. The creek was Manigault's Harvard and Yale, and he was free with its wisdom and largesse. Through him I learned where the conchs congregated, where the clams kept secret rendezvous, what holes hid the sweetest crabs, where oysters grew enormous and, one summer, how to read the creek for shrimp and mullet.

Manigault liked shrimp, and he and I skirmished over holes when we'd meet, he ascending Porcher's in his bateau, me descending in mine. He'd row standing up in his bateau, looking here and there for mudflats rich with shrimp, for holes only he knew where the shrimp congregated at low tide.

Daddy had taught me how to learn a creek's holes by casting where shrimpers like Manigualt cast. "Mark where he stops, boy, and next tide beat him out there. That man's forgotten more shrimp holes than you'll ever find." So I haunted his wake, floating a meander or two behind him, peering out from the marsh to watch him filling his buckets in a hole. I marked them, and beat him to them the next day. There I'd be, casting away in his best hole when he showed up. "Get along, boy, this here's my hole. I seen you following me yesterday, and today you out here stealing my shrimp." "I was here first; it's my hole." "Boy, there ain't room enough for the two of us in this hole, and I'm telling you this here is my hole. I got rights to it. Go on, get; give this here hole to someone who knows how to cast." Then he'd proceed to show me how to cast.

Out and up he'd throw his cotton net, blossoming in a gossamer circle bespangled with drops of water, like a spider's web flung against the sky. Out and up it would sail, higher and bigger than anything I'd ever thrown, and then it would fall, disappearing into the water like frost lines melting on a window pane, vanishing with a barely audible plop. A cast net's weighted perimeter is tied at intervals to an umbrella-like array of drawlines all tied to a cord that passes through a hole in the center of net to the caster's hand. As he pulls on the cord, it pulls the outer edge of the net; anything under the net larger than the mesh is caught in the purse formed by the net tucking in on itself.

Nets come in varying sizes. I learned on a net four feet in diameter, graduated to a six-footer, and am now happy with an eight-footer. An eight-foot net, if properly thrown, covers twelve and a half square feet of shrimp-filled water, a four-footer only half that. The larger the net, the more awkward to throw and the heavier.

Down in Florida they're said to heave twelve-foot nets. These must be made of fishing line; nobody could throw a twelve-foot cotton net all morning long. Machine-made nylon nets fetch thirty-five dollars in the big chain stores out on the bypass. They're safe enough if you don't cast near oysters, but show one an oyster, and you've got a hole the size of Lake Marion through which your catch escapes. If you shrimp holes the way I do, you can go through two or three such nets a season. The Japanese who make them are no doubt grateful, but I'd just as soon support the local firemen who weave cotton nets in their spare time. A handmade net costs over $100, is heavy as hell when wet, but lasts years.

Cast nets and shrimp were excuses to get out in the creek. Like my Virginia friends who spend fruitless morning after fruitless morning on deer stands, I find meat but a grownup excuse to be a boy again, free to go wherever my fancy takes me. Searching for the elusive super hole was excuse enough to float ever farther down Porcher's, past where it met Copahee, past where Gray's Bay flowed into it, to where Porcher's took on the grandeur of a river, flowing deep and barless between two banks a hundred feet apart. Fat with water and lazy, Porcher's wove her way through the marsh in ever broader meanders, long, looping bends and backbends the envy of any gymnast.

Smaller creeks debouched with regularity along both sides, each mouth calling to me. Entering such tributaries, I soon lost any sense of the larger creek, pushing my bateau up ever-narrower, ever-tighter curves playing loop the loop, bending back upon themselves like a pleated Christmas ribbon. Each creek had secrets to share with anyone who ventured up it. Like Cavalier de la Salle, I ventured up one, discovering hidden hole after hidden hole, secret troves of shrimp and mullet, known but to me and the otters I'd surprise fishing there. Were I quiet enough, I could watch them through a green screen of marsh sliding one after the other down the mud bank that overlooked their hole, splashing into the water, rising in a snort of bubbles and water, clambering up bank to start over again. Should they catch sight or scent of me, they were gone, up the mud bank and into the marsh, cutting cross-country to other marsh-bound channels that led them two miles back to land.

Pools quiet enough to be transparent sheltered groves of white and yellow and purple and orange whip coral, but too shallow to fish, held marvels worth a thousand shrimp. Stopping, I'd watch their dance and spy minute white blossoms blooming; these were the coral animals at dinner, seining the water with tentacles too small to see, building colors out of water, reaching towards the air like living skyscrapers designed and painted by Dr. Seuss. Storms rip them from their shelly substrate and they collect on beaches and point bars along creeks. No earth-borne flower's scent's as sweet as a bouquet of such sea blooms, rich with salt. I've a vase of them here in Virginia; I bury my nose in the sea-smelling salts and faint no more, their perfume as fresh as when I found them ten years ago. Defying Einstein, I travel instantaneously through space and time and stand again upon a distant shore.

An oyster bank sheltered behind its razored ramparts a pool of green anemones, creeky chrysanthemums whose petals wove spells of enchantment, luring me closer and closer until, nose dipping into water, I frightened myself and my anemones back to reality. Their tentacles vanished, and what had been weaving beauties became dull buttons. Wait, and, like Shelley's "sea-blooms and the oozy woods which wear/ The sapless foliage of the ocean," they bloomed again, fish rather than birds making their way through this water-feeding foliage.

An oak branch, ripped by some storm and carried here, had traded acorns for acorn barnacles, sprouting a hundred thousand along its barkless length. Those still beneath the water fluttered fan-like feet, or cirri, waving hapless plankton into their maws like sirens seducing sailors to their doom. Cobalt blue mussels crowded among the barnacles, and a dozen marsh fiddlers played king of the mountain on the branch's pinnacle.

A gypsy camp of wandering hermit crabs had squatted among the marsh's green trunks, each in a banded tulip shell of dubious provenance. Their shells were ill-kempt, covered with a scum of algae and the occasional barnacle; but they were borrowed houses, after all, each crab moving to a larger shell when he or she felt cramped. Daddy claimed they congregated only in certain places because they favored the taste of the creek just there; it spoke to them of carcasses, their favorite food. "Hermits are as choosy as some people about where they live," he explained. "They're partial to lightning whelks and tulips shells, maybe because they're all right-handed and need a shell that curls the way their bodies curl. It's God's curse upon you lefties; even Jesus sits on the right hand of the Almighty."

Farther up the creek, the marsh grass hung overhead in a green fretwork. My brother tells me the salt marsh outproduces the richest farmlands, growing up to nine tons of grass an acre, several times the best that Indiana corn fields can produce. Southern marshes are too boggy except at their edges to use as meadows. New England marshes, however, are built on a firm foundation, and colonists actually used them as pastures, grazing their cattle there and harvesting the marsh like hay (something I didn't believe until I'd walked out into a firm-under-foot Connecticut marsh). Grass is best for haying when it has headed up but hasn't yet matured. Northern marshes reach this stage sometime in August, and farmers would go out and cut them. Curing the hay in the sun, they would either carry it home or leave it stacked on platforms elevated above the tide.

Northern salt marsh is actually a different plant from southern salt marsh. Both are members of the *Spartina* genus, the northern grass being *S. patens*, our southern *S. alterniflora*. *S. patens* has both shorter and finer leaves than its cousin. When the two grow in the same area, *S. patens* takes the high ground, *S. alterniflora* the low.

S. alterniflora dominates Porcher's marshes. Near land it is stunted, only a foot or so high, growing on the broad sand flats which were our childhood highways. Firm, sandy, and open, it stretches as far as the eye can see both ways along the coast. I'd wander this marsh for hours, discovering among the tidal flotsam and jetsam childish treasures—fiddlers' claws, raccoon skulls thick and stubby, bird skulls lightweight and adorned with bills, egret mating feathers, white and airy as lace, opalescent mussel shells, a dozen different colored clays and sands, desiccated crab shells, entire and empty. Everywhere is man's trace— a recycling center's worth of bottles, cans and styrofoam.

This high marsh reminds nearly every visitor of the mythic West—nothing but green grass, interrupted perhaps by the blue glint of a creek, stretching for miles round the very curve of the earth itself, or framed on the far away horizon by a jagged line of trees marking the barrier islands. Above, the gloriously blue summer sky, "this brave o'erhanging firmament," fills the world like some wrap-around magni-cinema, with thunderheads building landward, and itself fading to blue-white nothingness in impossibly remote realms. Rising through shades of blue to unimaginable heights, high, higher, and even higher, the nearly invisible woodstorks, so faint and far off that they seem to be floating angels, lazily ride thermals out of this world and into another.

Before they headed west for Texas and glory, cowboys were black Carolinians, running dogies and fattening cattle in the high marsh. Hence the name cowboy: cow for the job and boy for the racial epithet, which was common at that time. My grandfather grazed cattle and sheep in the marshes, though by his day even the marsh had been fenced. My father can just remember when cattle roamed free, and fences were for keeping animals out. His daddy raised cattle and sheep in the marsh, and my daddy herded them. Here and there a row of drunken fence posts in the marsh recall when cattle grazed beneath the watchful eyes of boys now older than my venerable father.

Nowhere east of the Mississippi can you enjoy such magnitude as in the salt marsh, not even from the tops of a mountain. Although you may, technically, see farther from there than on the edge of a marsh, the precipice between you and all you view distances the world, frames it, makes it a picture. In the marsh, though, you are in the picture; it begins, there at your feet, and runs off as far and free and clean and new as anyone could wish.

The low marsh is another matter entirely. Six hours and a hundred feet from where you stood in the high marsh at high tide, the world narrows, circumscribed by green, and all you can see is green in front and in back, to the sides and overhead, a green screen of coarse-leafed grass closing in; only a narrow muddy ribbon of water to guide you through air palpable with heat, oppressive, cloying, clinging, still and rich with death, with the sweet, corrupt odor of rotting grass and rotting animals and rotting algae, tinged with a whiff of hydrogen sulfide seeping up from anaerobic muds two feet deep. Now the marsh is intimate, voluptuous, a living, decaying seductress out of Poe, tempting you ever farther up her devious course, a world cacophonous with life. The plopping of pistol shrimp, the croaking of herons, the splash of a mullet, the rustle of a thousand fleeing fiddlers, the scream of a marsh hen—myriad lives crackling and popping and snapping as they have for millennia.

The low marsh (low only in altitude above sea level) soars up to ten feet high; add two more feet of creek bank, and walking a narrow creek at low tide can be downright claustrophobic. The same marsh, at high tide, is a bucolic invitation. Now you glide through a thick-piled carpet of nodding, heavy headed grass that showers your gunwales with golden seed. Cavorting grasshoppers hitch rides and vault with insouciance across your bow, spiders' webs form stainless glass windows hung in the sky, the white-shelled turrets of periwinkles dangle from grass tips, marsh wrens' nests hang between grasses, and choirs of humming midges trail in your lee.

Of course, this is the marsh in good weather. Should your vocation require you to venture out in winter, Porcher's is less inviting. Cold, wet northeasters raise whitecaps in water so grey-green as to seem viscous, and Porcher's herself wrestles an ocean swell blown in from somewhere far north of Cape Hatteras. The sky lowers, as leaden as the water. The marsh, a withered driftwood grey, grows thin and sparse as a balding head. Low tide extends the sodden grey to mudbanks and oysterbeds, both covered in tattered sheets of algae. Winter water numbs feet and face and fingers, lungs ache with cold, and souls mildew and rot.

Gone are summer's scurrying fiddlers and popping shrimp, plopping mullet and cavorting grasshoppers. All are dead or swam south or east, seeking the warmth of ocean depths or Florida's shores. What life remains has hunkered down for the winter behind thick-shelled walls, and one begins to understand how winter hones the oyster razor thin and why the blue crab is as foul-tempered as a winter storm. Devoid of the planktonic hordes that clouded its summer depths, Porcher's grows translucent, as if viewed through a green bottle. After two or three months of this, just when it seems a new Ice Age is in the offing, one spies, from a dock or a boat, a school of fish, fifteen- or twenty-ten inch mullet just arrived from offshore. They drag along north Florida's warmth, waking the fiddlers still sleeping in the mud, and herding the shrimp into coastal waters. The mud, its algal coat shredded by feeding fish and fiddlers, basks in the still weak sun, and the marsh grass awakens, warmed from its winter slumber. New shoots wink fresh green as young asparagus, and Old Man Marsh sprouts new hair green as a teenaged punk's. My middle-aged hearing thaws, sharpens, and, at first faint and then louder, I hear the call of the creek, a clear call, a wild call, a call that cannot be denied. I must go down to Porcher's again.

2

Winter

In December, when Virginia is cold and barren and shrouded in snow, I migrate southward along the ancient track of birds and butterflies. Driving a hundred interstate miles up the Valley of Virginia, climbing a thousand feet in twenty miles to the New River Plateau, catching my breath sixty miles later at the thousand-foot-wall that is the Blue Ridge Escarpment, I look down on the rolling Piedmont and bid farewell to rhododendron, mountain laurel, hemlock and Virginia. At the bottom, I'll drive a hundred miles of North Carolina's pine woods and oak and hickory hills, watching for the first sweet gums to appear somewhere near the Yadkin River, watching cars gradually outnumber trees as I approach Charlotte. Another hundred miles in South Carolina, lanky loblollies will have supplanted stouter Virginia pines, and in a blue haze the Coastal Plain begins with a hilly hurrah in Columbia's Sand Hills.

Then the land and I calm down. I take the old two-lane road home now, winding out of the Sand Hills, remnants of sand dunes from a seashore vanished ten million years ago. Here, fifteen miles outside Columbia, oaks, bare-leafed and black, huddle forlornly round a swampy lake, wrapping themselves in coats of Spanish moss for warmth. Spanish moss—first sign that the land feels, even this far inland, the warm kiss of the sea. It's December and the pecan trees, pruned to a gracious Y, lift bare branches skyward in mute appeal for spring. Bedraggled cotton bolls hang unharvested in field after field, and last summer's corn stalks have collapsed.

The Coastal Plain takes a sedate hundred miles to drop eight hundred feet, though much of this descent's accomplished in a series of ten to twenty foot drops, escarpments where the receding sea paused for a hundred thousand years or more and then began its long withdrawal once again. Each creek I now cross runs clear and brown with tannin, through woods thick with vines and trees green the year round, into the immense swamps that still line the Congaree River and Four Hole Swamp. In protected pockets are remnants of the forest primeval that greeted the first Europeans—cypress and tupelo in whose dark depths Sarah, my wife, and I have watched white herons dancing in summer courtship. Green anoles with pink dewlaps do their lizardy come hither push-ups, stole-like serpents drape over branches, a dozen turtles vie for precarious perches on sodden logs, and bright yellow prothonotary warblers flit through the gloom from which we've run, tormented to madness by mosquitoes.

Thirty miles from the coast, giant dump trucks roar by in a cloud of dust twenty million years old, their cargo crushed limestone and fossil sharks' teeth, crabs, oysters and scallops. Forests of pines careen past, chained to the beds of logging trucks, subdivisions sprouting like fungi in their wake.

I retreat to the interstate and hold my nose as I pass the pulp and paper plant, a science fiction space station at night, reduced in daytime to a factory into whose maw hundreds of box cars roll, each brimming over with forests ground to sawdust for tomorrow's newspaper, grocery bag, this book. I roll over Daniel Island, its marshes diked and drowned under a sea of mud spewed up to make a channel for Navy ships that call no more. Ten years ago a sleepy farming island, Daniel is today an exit on the newly-built freeway whose high-arcing bridge over the Wando River provides a fleeting glimpse of a past so beautiful they should have built a turnout at the top so we could all take a long last look at the broad blue-green river flanked with carpets of greening grass in which creeks dance blue arabesques. Loblollies reach for cumulus clouds pillowed one atop the other, white as the cotton that once grew here, against a blue sky that fades finally into a haze you'd like to think the exhalation of trees, but one you know to be a brown haze of pollution so thick the future of this river cannot be descried.

A look down and to the right provides both a good look at what it might be and an explanation for why they built a bridge halfway to heaven—the spanking new State Ports Authority container terminal. It is a gigantic truck stop at the end of the interstate where round-the-clock monster cranes lift tractor trailers on and off ships so big they seem to duck when passing under the twin Cooper River bridges, frightening passengers in the cars riding overhead. Gone are the trim silhouettes of freighters like those my father shipped out on sixty years ago and whose arcana he taught us children; we'd cross the Cooper River bridge and look down upon the docks, learning to recognize Britain's Union Jack, the French tricolor, the Hellenic blues and whites of Greece, the crosses of Scandinavia, Turkey's crescent moon, Japan's red sun, and Korea's magic Tao sticks. He showed us star-studded captains' flags, taught us to tell a freighter's balanced silhouette from that of stern-heavy tankers, and both of these from the lean lines of destroyers. We knew to look for deep-drafted missile subs only on high tides, to guess how much cargo a ship carried by how she sat in the water, to dream like our father did of far away ports of call, to feel the bite of the North Sea in the Maersk Line's blue hulls and the tropic sun when we saw the banana boats' white hulls.

On the other side of the river, this far out, Highway 17 was a rural road forty years ago in my youth. Churches were once the loudest architecture here; Episcopalians, Presbyterians, Baptists, African Methodist Episcopalians competing for souls. The fields have since sprouted stores, the old packing shed where I crated tomatoes and cucumbers sells discount fabrics, each crossroads boasts a stoplight. Where I rode horses, today they hawk fried chicken, hamburgers, and tacos.

I take the road to my sister's house. Blue sewer pipes lie tumbled in the ditch; the public service authority's running sewer out here for developers. Without city sewer, lots must be an acre to handle septic systems; with city sewer, they can sell sixteenth-of-an-acre lots and put in apartment complexes. Billboards announce the glorious future: Ivy Hall, Victory Pointe, Charleston National. Finally I turn onto a dirt road and bounce my way a mile into the past. A snake sss-es across the dirt road ahead of me, blackberry briars slither into the median, a flock of egrets whitens the sky, and through the green-grey frame of live oaks, I spy my sister's house and the creek beyond.

Home again, or as close to it this side of death as I'll ever be, I walk down to the dock to clear my head of eight hours driving. I shed my Virginia sweater and pants for Carolina's shorts and shirt, and amble tennis-shoed down Porcher's Bluff's single sand lane. The houses are new, built since "the hundred-year-hurricane" Hugo in 1989 devastated the region. The families, all nine of them, are the same, having rebuilt in the same places as before. The old Porcher house survived the storm, the only house on the point to do so. So too did its gnarled live oaks and soaring palmettos; but the oaks, sixteen feet around at base, are naked, their Spanish moss blown halfway to Georgia by Hugo.

They had to build a new dock, of course. The old one was already decrepit when Hugo came. So worm-eaten were its out-of-kilter creosote posts, and so rotted the planks that sagged between them, that half the community refused to use the dock. Worse still, it was accessible by boat only at high tide, ending as it did in a muddy slough. The new dock is a wonder of pressure-treated planks and posts, solid and running straight as a forest road six hundred feet to midcreek. At high tide, it sticks so far out into water that you'd think it must be a walkway to the sea islands that some madman gave up on. Come low tide, though, you see it's a mud-mired marvel whose far end barely nuzzles the channel.

I sit on the end of the dock, listening to the water slapping against the posts. The tide is full, and Porcher's Creek winds bluely through its host, the marsh grass, spring's green already filling winter's faded brown stems. Across the creek, marooned in a halo of marsh, lies a dream isle, an Indian shell ring, palmettos rising evergreen and graceful along its beach, a live oak dipping its egret-clad branches into the water. Beyond that, Copahee Sound, a blue sheet of water stretches out its four-mile-long arms to embrace Dewee's and Caper's, barrier islands whose serried tree lines are a tropic silhouette of yet more palmettos.

Breathing slow and deep, I drink in air, absorbing the breath of the marsh, laden with salt and memories. I kneel, penitent, and dip my hands into the creek, my stoup, my font of holy water. I anoint myself, splashing my face and hair with water, washing away forty years of wandering in the wilderness. In a baptism of enthusiasm, knowing it's now or never, my salvation crying to me, I rise and hurl myself into the creek, gasping at its wintry embrace, drinking it as a tonic, gargling, rinsing, purifying myself of myself.

3

Stone Crabs

I ran into my childhood the other day in the grocery store's meat department. There, sandwiched between Alaskan king crabs and fake crab meat, were a jumble of stone crab claws. As a child, I made finger puppets out of empty stone crab claws. Thick and stubby, the rusty red claws curve like a bird's head and end in black-tipped pincers that resemble, to a child's imagination, a parrot's beak.

Down in Florida they catch stone crabs—like we catch blue crabs—in pots. My father caught them the old-fashioned way. He took a long, narrow coon oyster and knelt, very carefully, on the oyster bank. Then he felt his way into the burrow with the oyster until he encountered the crab. With luck, he found him halfway down the burrow where the walls were too narrow for him to open his claws. If so, he'd slide his oyster over the crab's back and coax him out, fast and smooth enough so he couldn't wedge himself against his burrow walls. Then he'd break off one claw and put the crab back in his burrow to grow another.

Sounds easier than it is, especially if you have to go so deep that you're lying down, nose in the mud, your hand and arm buried in a burrow and you still can't find him. Stone crabs burrow two feet and more into oyster banks, excavating a little room at the end of their burrow in which they sit, claws folded, waiting to see what drops in. You can tell an active hole by the fresh detritus piled up at its front door, white sand and fresh shell revealing what a busy housekeeper the crab is during high tide. At low tide his burrow remains flooded, a refuge for all sorts of animals—worms, fish, shrimp and crabs—some of which become stone crab dinner.

Stone crab claws are big things, up to two inches thick. Capable of cracking an oyster shell, or a finger. We never went stone crabbing alone. On the way out to Bull's Bay is Ghost Point, which got its name from a crabber who went out alone and never returned. Lying flat on the oyster bank, he stuck his arm down a crab hole and into the chamber; the crab grabbed hold of his finger and wouldn't let go. Facing out, the crab was too wide to fit through the burrow. Lying flat as he was, the crabber couldn't dig his way out with his other arm, either. Nothing to do but wait for someone to come by. Nobody did. The tide turned and started coming in. He could move his head a bit, hold his nose and mouth up out of the water for a while, but not for long enough. He drowned very slowly. Ghost Point was an object lesson for us each time our father took us out.

He showed us how to crab, but never let us do it. "Too dangerous," he'd say. "Wait until next year." Next year we heard the same excuse. So I taught myself to crab, surreptitiously, alone. I still don't have anyone to go crabbing with. It's enjoyable being alone; but splayed out, face down in the mud, oysters biting into my cheek, my left arm buried up to the shoulder, and the tide rising, I recollect Ghost Point and wonder if I'm as big a God-damned fool as I must look to the herons.

Stone crab burrows are surprisingly smooth-walled for being muddy holes in oyster banks. Even at low tide, they are filled with water, providing shelter for not only stone crabs, but also toad and oyster fish, worms, and mud crabs. Reaching in with a coon oyster in place of an eye, I can feel dead oyster shells along the soft underbelly of my forearm; reaching deeper, I pin my biceps against the still-living barricade of oysters that surrounds the hole and know that if I haven't reached the crab by now, I won't. With experience, the way an oyster shell slides up and over the carapace betrays a crab's presence. Hunched in his hole like a curmudgeonly hermit, the stone crab cannot grab hold of your fingers, at least in theory. Some burrows end in chambers spacious enough for a crab to stretch out in; some burrows, dug by large crabs, have been inherited by smaller crabs. Some are inhabited by things other than crabs; the local College of Charleston has in formaldehyde an octopus my father yanked out of a stone crab hole forty years ago. Feeling a crab wedged sideways in its burrow, I reach over and behind it with the shell and scoot it up and out of the hole.

I steal the larger claw. Fresh stone crab is a dinner too good to share with anyone but kin, and impossible to find two hundred miles inland. So here, in

Virginia, I bought some frozen claws, knowing in advance I shouldn't, took them home, steamed them, picked out the largest and best and broke it open with a pair of pliers, extracted its meat and savored my childhood—hard and dry and freezer-burned from too long a storage.

4

Conchs

Every child knows what we grownups forget; conchs conjure the sea they came from. No matter how far inland you be, hold an empty conch to your ear and you will hear the faint, far-off sound of the surf upon the conch's natal beach. Sarah has been around the world, and brought back conchs from the South Pacific and the Caribbean. When the workaday world of Virginia gets too much, we escape to Bora Bora, holding to each ear a conch, hearing the Pacific in stereo.

Science insists these seas are but ourselves, the roar of our blood magnified in the conch's sounding box and echoed back to the ear whence it came. So be it; what greater seas than those within, before which the Pacific in all its magnitude is but the Gulf of Mexico, a Porcher's Creek to the Gulf Stream of myself?

Isaac Newton supposed himself a child upon such a seashore, gravity and the laws of motion gaudy seashells cast up from a far greater mystery of which he was but dimly aware. We are all shellers on our own internal oceans, picking up this and that broken, partial, or nearly perfect castoff from depths we fear to wade into. If this skeleton jetsam fascinates, what living marvels hide beneath the waves?

Porcher's lower reaches are home to conchs. They clamber over oyster and clam beds, dining on sleepy bivalves between whose yawning shells they insinuate their feet like unwelcome door-to-door salesmen. Locked out, they beat their way in, hammering the shells' edges until they fracture. Once in, they eat alive their host or hostess. From such meals conchs fashion their shells, opalescent orange and purple in Carolina's waters.

What you may well call a whelk, I call a conch. The conch's operculum—the horny oval it closes its shell with—has been so modified that it resembles more a claw than the flat oval whelks crawl about on. My "conchs" have flat opercula; hence, they're whelks, according to the scientists, who need words that mean the same thing everywhere. Regional pride requires that I second Lewis Carroll's Humpty Dumpty, who sagely observed, "When I use a word, it means just what I choose it to mean—neither more nor less." They're conchs, by God.

Whelk or conch: an aphrodisiac by any other name would still sweeten old men's nights. Oysters have long been supposed aphrodisiacs but, as one fisherman told me, "the oyster, he good. But the conch, he better. 'Cause the conch, he eat the oyster." The conch's muscular foot is an organ designed to impress—or depress—a dirty old man. Catch one afoot in the creek and pick him up; he'll piss all over you as he dehydrates into his shell. Touch him before he disappears behind his operculum; that's one tough, meaty muscle, much admired by those whose muscular feet droop.

Like drooping feet, a conch's meat must be beaten to be useful. The *Joy of Cooking* instructs one to tenderize a conch by putting it in a canvas bag and pulverizing it. The best way to eat a conch, though, is like the Bahamians do it: gouge a hole in the spike end of the shell, cut his foot off, and pull him out the front door. Cut off the operculum, chop the rest into pieces with a cleaver, add diced onion and tomato, and cook him in lemon juice.

Porcher's Indians cut conchs out the same way. Their mounds are full of conch shells with holes cut in their upper ends. Age has bleached these conch bones white. For whole shells, still flushed orange and purple, you have to go to the beach.

Beaches are graveyards of the creek and sea. Each shell is its occupant's cenotaph, each beach littered with empty tombs; it is always Easter morning on the world's seashores. What an unglorious resurrection, though, to rise translated into a conch. Cannibals, they eat their own kind to make their homes, the slime of sea snails transmogrified into orange and purple, pink and green, white and black contortions we call shells.

To what bizarre ends we employ the deaths of others. My grandmother knew a beach of skulls on Morris Island, off Charleston Harbor, south of

Porcher's. Its lighthouse, abandoned today, watched shrimp boats trawl where my grandmother strolled a hundred years ago. The beach was littered then, she said, with human bones, leg bones and arm bones, vertebrae, occasional skulls, all washed smooth and white by the dicing sea.

Having sailed out from the city, my grandmother and her wooer would spend a long afternoon on this islanded edge of the New World, gathering shells and waiting for evening. Flirting with each other, they'd look across the harbor channel to Sullivan's Island and Fort Moultrie where Edgar Allen Poe, an enlisted man in the U.S. Army, had stood eighty years before and stared out at an unreachable Morris Island, thinking of an equally unattainable Annabel Lee. Between him and my grandmother lay fifty years and Fort Sumter, the Civil War, and a ditch full of dead men emptying itself onto a beach. Now I, voyeur, stand beside them, listening to a long-dead lover seduce my mother's mother with lines I too will use, "And so, all the night-tide, I lie down by the side/ Of my darling, my darling, my life and my bride,/ In her sepulchre there by the sea —/ In her tomb by the side of the sea."

My grandmother's skirts caressed the bones of the 54th Massachusetts, a black regiment commanded by white officers, who died attacking Battery Wagner, a Southern fort that guarded Fort Sumter. Whites and blacks were unceremoniously buried together in the Battery's defensive ditch, such integration presumed by the Confederates to be an insult to the whites. Today the 54th marches in bronzed ranks across a monument on the Boston Common, led by its white commander, Colonel Robert Gould Shaw. Poet Robert Lowell claimed "Shaw's father wanted no monument/except the ditch,/ where his son's body was thrown/ and lost with his 'niggers.' "

Lost only for so long, however. Hart Crane knew what becomes of "the dice of drowned men's bones." Conchs eat them, or eat that which eats them, sucking calcium from white and black, Yankee and Rebel, building coiled castles from the dead, "the portent wound in corridors of shells."

My grandmother heard a water-washed echo of July 18, 1863, the dull roar of wave and cannon mingling with her blood's roar as her lucky lover pressed a conch shell to her ear, his lips to her lips; dim, ever so dim, my grandmother's lover whispering Poe to her on a moonlit beach.

Ghost soldiers died and screamed round me as she pressed to my ear the same conch. "Listen," she said, "you can hear the sea and the sound of cannon." I did. I do.

5

Fiddlers

So crowded and noisy are fiddler colonies that I could hear the crabs eating long before I saw them. Swimming toward a summer mud bank, only my head exposed, ever so slowly I'd beach myself with the sun in my eyes so I didn't stand out against the horizon that two thousand stalked eyes watched. I'd listen to a thousand maws munching mud against a background symphony of splashing mullet and popping shrimp. An incautious move and, swoosh, with a sound like wind in spring leaves, the bank emptied. A thousand holes remained, some large, some small, some crowded, some off to themselves, for all the world like birdshot patterns in a rural roadsign.

Thirty or forty seconds would pass, and then the braver crabs would re-emerge, burrows sprouting pink-elbowed claws that pushed their way sunward, edgy and ready to retreat at the least provocation. Their numbers swelled until each burrow sported a male waving an enormous arm after whose antics the crab is named. A thousand frantic elbows fiddled on my mud bank alone. A symphony echoed on both sides of the creek where twice four miles of fiddlers practiced notes from me to the sea—on a continental shoreline dotted with creeks. No one knows just how many fiddlers there are in the world, but some estimate they number more than a million an acre.

Each male crab bears what all marsh visitors recall, a disproportionately large claw. It can weigh up to fifty percent of a crab's total bodyweight. This massive appendage intrigued Darwin, who considered it a crustacean equivalent to the peacock's tail, the Irish elk's antlers, the bird-of-paradise's tailfeathers, the human male's pumped up biceps.

Such mad male plumage is hardly the product of natural selection, which is supposed to *increase* one's survival chances. A male fiddler can't even eat with his claw. Watch a bank: the females feed with both claws, stuffing mud and meal—minute plants and animals and detritus—down their gullets, drooling gobbets of wet mud that pile up beneath their jaws. The males, just as hungry but condemned to carry gargantuan claws, shovel muck with one claw twice as fast as the females in order to keep up at the buffet.

In *The Descent of Man*, Darwin suggested such handicaps evolve because of sexual selection, the result of millennia of female crabs preferring Billy's big claw to Bobby's lesser appendage. Sexual selection is supposed to handicap one's survival chances; if I can carry around a seventy-five-pound left arm and still manage to feed and clothe myself and build a lovely mud hut, just think what advantages our children will have. Make it with me, and our boys will have the same great claws, antlers, tails, biceps, whatever turns you on. Our girls, of course, will have whatever outstanding secondary sexual characteristics first caught my male fantasy.

Successful fiddling convinces a passing female to spend the tide with her lucky crab. What to a female is a come-hither, however, is to another male is an offer to fight. Each burrow-bound bravo engages in suburban border disputes with his neighbors, each trying to sneak his property line another millimeter farther onto his neighbor's turf. Since the fiddler is both gregarious and pugnacious, border wars are interminable. It's mine. It isn't. Is. Isn't. Is. Isn't. Each burrow has some four neighbors, each neighbor four neighbors in turn, a bellum omnia contra omnes, a war of all against all, and the devil take the hindmost. While he patrols his eastern flank, his western borders crumble; shore them up, and the south flank lies exposed; and so all low tide long.

Here and there are wandering males, looking for a fight. Give me your burrow or else, they signal furiously with their claws. You and whose army, retorts the proud possessor. Thus ensues a highly stylized battle, claws pressed into service as epees, as battle axes, the clash of carapace on carapace—armored knights battling for an inverted castle keep and a fair female's claw.

What seems at first mad confusion is, in fact, as ordered as a fencing tournament, each aggressive move as ritualized as the response it evokes. Mud-mired observers have counted a dozen different thrusts, an equal number of parries, even a sequence of thrust-parry-thrust. One has written the illustrated guide to fiddlers' fencing. Like human matches, these matches seldom result in dismemberment or death. Indeed, what might appear relentless warfare, a nasty, brutish, and brief Hobbesian nightmare of continuous battle, resolves itself without a death. The winner gains at most a burrow, the loser moving down the beach to find some smaller unfortunate to kick out in turn until the smallest one gives up and hides beneath a shell.

Helen of Troy caused no greater turmoil than do the wandering women of the fiddler colony. Let one parade herself down muscle beach, and watch the males go to it, flexing their claws with a come-hither-honey bravado, as often as not ignored.

She's as fickle as Helen, too. Any colony of crabs scared into hiding will have a scattering of holes from which careless elbows extrude, the elbows of males who have gallantly offered their burrows as refuge to homeless damsel fiddlers in distress. Such careless elbows are a crab cocktail for foraging herons, who grab the elbow in their beak and pull the hapless crab out, jerking him till his body breaks off from the huge claw, which the bird jettisons in favor of the now defenseless crab. Every mudflat generally sports a couple of these sad tokens by the turning of the tide. Meanwhile the damsel for whom the anonymous crab died has clambered down another burrow, where she fiddles around for another six hours a foot below ground. Plugged holes at low tide hide couples too intent on lovemaking to eat; dig down and you'll scare them out.

Porcher's two kinds of fiddlers have divided their territory by substrate. Sand fiddlers—*Uca pugilator*—plug their burrows because the rising water would collapse them if the trapped air did not provide a counterforce. Mud fiddlers—*Uca pugnax*—having chosen a stickier building material, prefer an open door policy. They even construct chimneys reminiscent of those crawfish build, chimneys some scientists theorize serve as band shells against which they silhouette their fiddling. Mud fiddlers are big, blue-green crabs whose huge-clawed males resemble big city punks looking for a fight. Sand fiddlers are dainty, diminutive crabs better known as China-backed fiddlers, after the mottled purple-pink pattern on their backs reminiscent of a China doll's floral tea service.

Both species' names suggest a bellicose nature. Who can't help but admire an inch-long crab that hoists itself up on spread legs, and waves its claw defiantly at all comers-on, even bipedal monsters six feet tall? Midsummer fiddlers are way too sprightly to be caught by any but the quickest of humans. Summer colonies vanish in an instant whenever any motion, even a passing cloud, threatens. Six months later, even the slowest of us can catch them soaking up the weak rays of the winter sun. Fiddlers hibernate but, as far south as Carolina, those living in the high marsh will emerge on warm winter days. Those living farther down in the creek, however, stay hidden all winter long. Where lesser mortals look to robins to announce spring, Carolinians attend the yearly resurrection of the fiddler. One day a grey, unbroken expanse of mud, the next day the marsh is alive with fiddlers constructing tiny towers, the muddy verge turned over like a disked field where foraging raccoons plowed all night long for fiddlers.

In winter, ungrazed, the fiddler's food—algae in the mudbanks—proliferates, and summer's grey sheet is replaced by winter's green blanket. Summer mudbanks emerge water-smoothed and grey, but by tide's turn they become unmade, dirty grey sheets spotted with fiddlers' tracks, dotted with their holes. Once they come out of their sand-plugged burrows, fiddlers spend a great deal of time housekeeping, trundling away sand in bundles between their legs, their holes finally coming to resemble rayed craters on the moon, each detritus-laden trip out a trajectory etched in sand. I have spent hours watching them cleaning up, the busy househusband poking his head out his burrow, clambering out sideways with his burden tucked between his eight legs, scuttling sideways to his junkyard's edge. You can judge how long a bank's been out of water by observing how thick these trajectories lie around the burrows; the more there are, the lower the tide. When the tide returns, the fiddlers retreat into their one- to two-foot-deep burrows, plugging them with sand and waiting six hours until they begin the process all over again.

Fiddler is an Americanism, there being no such creatures in the British Isles. Colonial explorer John Lawson, who passed by Porcher's in a dugout canoe on his way north, first used the term in 1709, writing that "Fidlars are a sort of small Crabs, that lie in Holes in the Marshes. The Raccoons eat them very much. I never knew any one try whether they were good Meat or no." There are Old World fiddler crabs, but they only range as far north as the Iberian peninsula, where their claws are eaten as hors d'oeuvres. The Japanese like fiddler claws so much they even can and sell them commercially. I've tried their claws boiled, but never found the small amount of meat worth the picking or the burden of their murder. Americans do buy and sell them— as bait and for research. Since the Northeast has pretty much bulldozed its marshes—and hence its fiddlers—into extinction, Yankee fishermen must look to Florida, where Southern fiddlers still wander the creek banks in droves. You can even buy fiddlers over the Internet, although these are for research, sold individually at ridiculous prices to scientists looking for the perfect laboratory animal.

Southern fiddlers are more gregarious than their northern relatives. Some of ours "herd," roaming the lowtide creeks with nary a burrow to hide in. As a child, I would stand still and listen to the rustle of fiddlers crawling under the marsh wrack. Slowly they would emerge, cautiously moving along the sandy bank. When a hundred, two hundred, a thousand fiddlers had forsaken safety for dinner, I'd flap my arms, jump, and they'd stampede, scuttling towards their marsh haven, the wrack heaving with their frenzied rush beneath it. I'd read of buffalo stampedes, of thousands of beasts rushing headlong off cliffs to die upon the rocks a hundred feet below. So too the fiddlers rushed headlong off creek banks, falling three feet to the sandy bottom, piling up in slopes of living talus which soon enough resolved again into individual fiddlers that picked themselves up and scurried off.

6

Porpoise

Porpoise know which holes are good to fish. They come up Porcher's alone or in groups at half tide to hunt the holes, never going farther upstream from the Bluff's dock than a quarter of a mile. Here lies a large hole, half as big as a football field, and deep enough that I've never hit bottom, a sort of discount fish store for enterprising porpoise.

My sister and brother and I remember the sound and sight of a school of porpoise hunting a hole, five or six huge beasts racing in circles, herding the fish in ever tighter circles. Our father let our bateau drift into their midst; he wanted to fish while the fishing was good. Porpoise to left of us, porpoise to right, maddened mullet throwing themselves unwittingly into our boat, and we ourselves wet with spray from the thrashing and splashing of fish and cetacean. One porpoise threw itself up on the mud bank, rolling out of the water, carrying with it a dozen mullet.

Porpoise—or Atlantic bottlenose dolphin as the scientists know them—eat over forty different kinds of fish. Silver perch, croaker, gray trout, mullet, and spot top the list, though toadfish, scorpionfish, and small sharks are known to be eaten, as well as squid, crab, and shrimp. Fishermen report porpoise taking mackerel, tarpon, sailfish, ray, mullet, catfish, and sheepshead from their lines!

These beasts are big. Should I catch one upstream of myself, he'll dive, moving faster than I supposed possible, and slip by within feet, his passage betrayed by a wake. Nuclear subs used to leave such wakes when they entered and left Charleston Harbor. So too the porpoise passes, a bullet-like deformation of the water's surface. Not a sound, nothing solid, just water molded to an underwater passage.

Porpoise regularly fish with humans. Mauritanian fishermen in North Africa summon them by beating the water; the porpoise then herd mullet schools close inshore where the fishermen can net them. Australian aborigines are said to have done the same sort of thing. Porpoise to this day on the Amazon, the Ganges, the Irrawaddy, and the Yangtse Rivers are said to herd fish for humans.

Once upon a time, one fished with me. He used to fish the same tributary I fished. I had mullet to spare and, one day, as he finished his fishing and turned to swim out, I threw him several. They disappeared into the depths and never rose. He left. During the next day and the next, for a week and more, we fished together. On the third day he lingered. We achieved, I like to think, a rapport. He'd precede me up "our" creek to where it ended in a muddy, shallow hole alive with fish. There he'd circle several times, herding mullet. I was busy casting behind him at the fear-maddened mullet that fled downstream. Then he would turn and cruise serenely downstream towards the main channel of Porcher's. I could feed him easily then, throwing several mullet out into the narrow creek and then, shortcutting across a peninsula, catch him as he turned upcreek in the main channel. He had his routine, holes that he visited every day. Safe in midchannel, he'd watch me, head half out of the water with that come-hither smile they all have.

He never came close enough to touch, however, which is what one can do with the ocean-going porpoise that sport about the bows of ships. My cousin's father used to take us deep-sea fishing. On the long ride out to the Gulf Stream, we children would lie stretched out on the bow, waiting for the dappled porpoise of the deep to come barreling skyward towards us. Offshore, the water is so clear we could see them rising at us from far below, up, up, and up till they broke the surface and jumped, effortlessly it seemed, ahead of the rushing boat, and disappeared into the depths, only to rise again and repeat the game. If we waited long enough, and were lucky enough, we could stroke them as they jumped, and tell ourselves they were letting us.

Why porpoise ride bow waves no one knows for sure. They surf not only ships and boats, but also whales. Some say it's sport; others maintain it conserves energy. Whose explanation you adopt reveals just how serious you think life is: do animals "play," or was Hobbes right about life being nasty, brutish and short?

There was another porpoise off Sullivan's that used to let us pet it, so tame had it become. It fished a large gully that led into the inlet between Sullivan's and the Isle of Palms, one island south of Porcher's. Good fishing there, for human and porpoise. Over time, it became accustomed to mankind, and would no longer flee, and, finally, towards the end of one summer, would actually brush against us children, its huge body, longer and heavier by far than ours, slowing to let us rub it.

One hundred and fifty pounds, six to eight feet of alien flesh brushing against a child makes him realize how frail his body really is. I remember fright in the presence of such power. With friends ashore, I couldn't not go out. Waist deep, then chest deep in water, fear and awe playing one against the other, as my toes slipped off and on the steeply shelving edge of the channel, I watched the grey beast grow closer and closer, impossibly larger and larger. I remember the grey flank and white belly, the watery, rubbery feel of skin unlike anything else that came out of water. The sidelong glance, the unintended smile, the eye, three times larger than mine.

A porpoise's sideways gaze betrays that he probably doesn't have binocular vision, that his eyes operate independently of each other. What might such a world look like, each eye sending back its own separate reality, and sonar yet another? Is his picture of the underwater world akin to the sonograms they make of human babies in the hospital? Am I a grainy black and white motion picture to him, my legs cut off at the waist where they disappear into the air? Does he surface simply to complete his picture? Does he see in color, hear in black and white? Might the water be his Kansas and the air his Oz?

We, too, use multiple senses to navigate by. My spirits lift when, homeward bound, I smell the sea; science claims it's ozone and salt I'm sniffing, my heart tells me it's home. We all judge distance by sound, whether listening to Canada geese honk overhead or counting seconds between lightning and thunder. We judge how close we are to the fire by feel.

We trust porpoise, of course. Both Plinys recorded friendships between porpoise and children, Pliny the Elder asserting that, so close were a dolphin and boy, the dolphin died of grief following his young friend's death. "Donald" in the Irish Sea, "Simo" off Wales, "Dolly" and "Georgie Girl" off Florida,

"Opo" off New Zealand, "Jean-Louis" off Brittany, "Dobbie" in the Red Sea have all played with humans in the last thirty years.

Not all porpoise are as trusting. One summer a mother porpoise frequented Porcher's Creek with her child. The child was its mother made small. Beautiful gun metal blue sides and back, fish belly white beneath, and a skin smooth and unscarred. The mother, like every grown-up I've ever seen, had her fair share of scars and scratches. My father told us these were scars from shark fights. When I was young, people said porpoise nearby meant there were no sharks. It ain't necessarily so, however, according to those who know; porpoise and shark both hunt the same fish, oftentimes at the same time. Other porpoise fighting porpoise, not sharks, probably cause most of the scars.

While the mother didn't shy away, she kept herself between me and her child. The two would appear together, peacefully cruising upstream, her child riding so close to her side as to appear as an appendage. They swam in unison and breathed in unison. Mother and child, cetacean rite of passage. No doubt, I imagined, she showed it her favorite holes, her secret shortcuts, much as I do my own son these days. I was intruder on this idyll, and destroyed it several times, chasing them off, mother always positioning herself between me and her child. Once I chanced to come between them, entering from a side creek. That time, the mother turned, rose on her tail out of the water as if at a Sea World show, squeaking loudly to her child, who squeaked and dove, swimming by and past me within three feet. In time, the mother grew accustomed to me, and would fish the larger creeks and holes along with me, though we were never friends enough for her to trust her child to a stranger.

Porpoise mothers do love their children, caring for them for several years. Australian researchers watched one mother mourning her dead child; she circled its floating body for hours in a lonely wake. Not all porpoise are as high-minded as this mother; three males finally drove her off with their unwanted sexual advances.

Copulation is preceded by "courtship," which involves a variety of sexual behaviors, including flashing the belly, rubbing the intended's genital area with body, beak, or penis. Porpoise have also been known to try to copulate with human divers and Zodiak rubber boats.

The porpoise penis hides in a genital groove located a couple of inches in front of the male's anal opening. Since the genital and anal slits are one and the same in female porpoise, this separation of the two in males is the most obvious way to sex a porpoise—if you can get close enough to do so. A porpoise penis is both longer and bigger round than a human penis; broad-based, it resembles a miniature elephant trunk, having a distinct curve to its tapered end. That tapered end fits into the female genital slit, which is marvelously adapted to copulation in the sea. Since salt water is lethal to sperm, the porpoise vagina has evolved a muscular "pseudocervix" capable of closing off the upper vagina. Some experts theorize that the tapered penis, having penetrated high up the vagina, withdraws, triggering vaginal muscles to contract, thus sheltering the just-deposited sperm in the upper vaginal tract. Perhaps this regular orgasm explains the porpoise's perpetual smile?

If you need porpoise, obviously it makes sense to breed them. Especially if you want ones predisposed to balance balls for tourists, seek out bombs for the Navy, whatever. Hence artificial insemination has become an item in Sea Worlds everywhere. Trainers teach their male porpoise to cooperate in this; it took one group fifty-five days to train their porpoise to "extend his penis on command," a trait some human males might envy. Twice a week, participating porpoise ejaculated during twenty to thirty minute "sessions." They came from once to a mighty twelve times a session, ejaculating between 0.1 and 39.5 ml at a time.

Humans do more than masturbate porpoise; they also hunt them. Europeans used to eat them in the Middle Ages. Queen Elizabeth I of England so loved porpoise meat she declared all porpoise caught in England "the queen's fish." Okinawans herd porpoise into a shallow bay and butcher them for meat. We Americans also eat porpoise, albeit inadvertently; tens of thousands drown each year in tuna nets and end up as canned "tuna." We trap, or used to trap, porpoise. That's where the commercial marinas once got all—and still get some—of their "performers."

Over five hundred thirty porpoise are known to have been "permanently removed" from the Gulf and Atlantic Coasts from 1973 to 1988. That's some thirty-three a year, with at least fifty-six in 1988 alone. This trapping is defined as a "fishery," which means it can be fished, but the government imposes limits. All those taken are, of course, for "research"; no one's going to give you or me a license to fish porpoise, although what's research to a Sea World in search of dollars, a navy in search of bombs, a doctor in search of cadavers, may not be your and my definition of research.

It used to be you didn't need a license. Not long ago there was a white porpoise who lived near Beaufort, South Carolina, and ran with her kind. Free, contented, one supposes. The media learned of her, and then the Sea Worlds did too. They came to hunt her. The county and then the state declared her off limits to such hunters, but South Carolina has no navy, so the Florida firms hunted her out to sea, out to international waters, chasing her mercilessly, exhausting her, cutting her off from her family, her school, eventually trapping her. They took her into permanent exile. They "trained" her as their freak slave and wrote "scholarly" articles on her. We paid plenty to see her; who wouldn't pay to see a white slave? She died, pining away perhaps for her vanished children, her vanished freedom. The company, of course, erected a plaque to her memory, although it never drew as many visitors as it had when she was alive.

You hear things if you stay long enough on the creek. She was not the only one of her kind, but fishermen no longer talk of what they see except in whispers, snatches of conversation held low and private, knowing to what lengths free enterprise will go to enslave the sea itself. Where, you ask, are the others? Somewhere between Virginia's Cape Henry and Florida's Cape Canaveral. More specific I will not be, but they are there.

7

Oysters

Oysters made Porcher's Bluff. People living here, black, red, and white, have carted oysters by the boatload landward for more than four thousand years, inadvertently building bluffs and entire islands in the process. Indians in dugout canoes made from hollowing out huge cypress trees first floated out to Copahee Sound and Gray's Bay on the outgoing tide to harvest the oysters that grow there on islands visible only at low tide. These oyster-studded islands scattered about for miles like pieces of a monstrous jigsaw puzzle. They returned home with the rising tide, threading their way through green-lined ribbons of water to high land, and their villages overlooking the creek and sound.

What was then land is now marsh, and the village sites themselves are today palmetto-rimmed islands whose top two feet are a rampart of oysters and clams and periwinkles dined on four millennia ago. Scattered throughout the shells are pottery shards, remnants of careless moments long forgot. The fired clay of these shards preserves lunate designs made with fingernails pressed into still damp clay, designs a modern fingernail fits perfectly. Indeed, they're known by some as "Awendaw fingerpinch." As children, we used to plunder these islands, carrying away booty to childhood museums. Always when we placed our fingernails in those crescents made so long ago by tribes unknown, we paused and stared with holy dread at each other. Even today, barred by age and law from stealing relics from what are now officially-declared state historic sites, I can reach into a drawer and pull out a water-worn fragment of pottery and fit my forefinger to an impression made by another forefinger long before the capitals of Europe were a dream, before Jerusalem, as old as the pyramids of Egypt.

Archeologists have excavated these shell middens, and say that these unknown villagers four, perhaps five, millennia ago were the first along these coasts to have oyster roasts. In a southern version of the New England clambake, villagers built fires in pits on whose coals they laid oysters and clams covered with marsh wrack to steam them open. Four thousand years later, we are still roasting oysters. Today we use above-ground fires, lay the oysters out on metal sheets, and cover them with wet gunny sacks to steam them open; or used to, as gunny sacks today are made of plastic, we're often reduced to using beach towels.

The Porchers used to have a church oyster roast every winter, harvesting oysters from beds they owned in Copahee. Many a time my family went with them. Winter oystering is a hard, cold, and muddy business in Copahee. The brilliant blue skies of Canadian cold fronts bring with them temperatures that mock the tropical silhouettes of palmettos we passed on the way to the oyster beds. Wet east winds whistle in straight off the winter Atlantic; the water turns green-grey and cold, the marsh grass, dying, fades brown, then grey, and the sky lowers, growing as grey and bleak as the oyster beds themselves. The only color anywhere is in foul weather gear, through whose rips and seams the pelting rain, blowing horizontally, seeps, soaking and chilling us.

The Project, the Porchers' converted shrimp boat, would pick its way through the maze of oyster-studded islands to a likely looking cove. We'd anchor, row out to a nearby bank, crunch ashore on an oyster paved beach, and begin our harvest. With sodden gloves and cold fingers, we picked through the rubble of loose oysters near low water. Oysters clung to oysters in a mockery of the Kama Sutra, ten or twenty shells glued one to the other in every conceivable combination. We searched for singles, oysters without partners, because these are larger and sweeter to eat. This was no singles bar, however, and we were reduced to splitting apart the hard-shelled, awkward clusters that were surprisingly fragile, though menacingly sharp.

It takes one hundred to one hundred and fifty Copahee oysters to fill a bushel gunny sack. A well-shaped oyster may be three or four inches long, an inch or two wide—small by many standards, but saltier and sweeter than anything you'll ever buy in store or restaurant. An oyster this size may be four or five years old. Older ones can get up to a foot in length but, in Copahee, by that time they're misshapen and hidden under a shell-breaking burden of pig-gybacking younger oysters. Crowded, like miniature Manhattans, clustering oysters have no way to grow but up. Eventually, the cluster sinks under its own weight, the original oyster, long since tortured into an arthritic-looking, elon-gated and meatless finger, suffocated in mud. His only consolation is that his piggybacking freeloaders will suffocate in turn.

The interior of a well-developed bed is nearly solid oysters, several thou-sand shells packed like standing knives so close together they seem pavement intended for a promenade. It's tempting to collect the long, slender oysters that grow here, but these "coon" oysters, as Daddy named them, have too little meat within to bother with. A good eating oyster has to have some girth to his shell, and coon oysters, though long, are notoriously skinny. Like Shake-speare's Julius Caesar, gourmets prefer fat companions: "let me have 'oysters' round me that are fat,/ sleek-shelled 'oysters,' such that sleep a-night." Every oyster has one shell more curved than the other; the bigger the bulge, the fat-ter and sweeter the meat within.

While the rich in New York City dine on oysters by the dozen, in Caro-lina, rich or poor, we eat them by the bushel. I can close my eyes now and see the white wooden tables in rows, each in its own circle of light cast by a naked light bulb on a cord running from branch to branch of the moss hung live oaks. At the far end of the tables, the silhouettes of lanky men gather around the roasting fires, some stoking them, some shoveling oysters, some jawing and drinking. Big boned, bosomy women keep towels and knives sup-plied to the rest, who shuck and eat, shuck and jive. I hold fast to my father's pants leg; he feeds me oysters, warm and dripping, from the end of his oyster knife. I taste from forty years ago the rusty knife, and the crunch of shell and mud competing with the salt of oysters.

These days we roast oysters in pans in the oven. My father sits at my sis-ter's table, and it is I who feed him, opening shells he can barely see now, cut-ting the adductor muscle that holds the oyster to its shell, and laying it on his plate. Take, eat; do this in memory of me. Tonight's ritual is a sacrament. Does he, like me, remember his father feeding him oysters, remember feeding his father, generation preceding generation, back to the beginning in a muddy laying on of hands?

"This is how you hold an oyster, son," Daddy said so many years, so many oysters, ago, turning my oyster round so that its bulging side is cradled in my glove-clad hand. "This is how you open it," he says, slipping an oyster knife expertly between the shells, slightly agape and hot after roasting. Prying off the upper shell, he cut the single muscle holding in the oyster and freed my hand. "God gave the oyster his own soup bowl, so you could slurp him down, juice and all."

"Ouch." "Here, let me help you with that." I am ten years older now, my own shucker of oysters, and in love with the girl standing next to me who has just cut her finger on an oyster. "Here. Let me see your finger." "It's nothing." "I know, but you should clean it out." She raises a beautiful hand towards me; a red line as fine and sweet as a honeysuckle's anther decorates her forefinger, widens, blossoms with nectar. I raise her hand to my mouth and kiss it; blood, salt, and mud mingle deliciously, seductively on my tongue. We look into each other's eyes, heads almost touching, her long hair tickling my face, scent of shampoo mingling with that of wood smoke and oyster.

Teenaged oyster roasts are sensual delights, shucking oysters an excuse for flirting. Having eaten your fill, there is always the water's edge to stand on, arms round each other, the moon glittering on the full basin of Copahee at high tide, and a soft sea breeze rustling the palmetto fronds and swaying the Spanish moss. From behind you through the dark come the voices of those still eating, occasional high bursts of laughter. Here too your father stood in his day; here have stood for as long as anyone remembers each generation's lovers, handing down through the years the arts of oystering and love.

"Eat fish, live longer; eat oysters, love longer." How oysters came to be aphrodisiacs no one seems to know. Nor, if my utterly unscientific polls of oyster-eaters be at all accurate, do oysters in fact have any observable effect on performance. The indecent intimacy of a raw oyster lying pooled in its own juices, the salt smell and sticky feel and off-white color reminiscent of seminal fluid, the excuse to touch each other, feed each other, are all suggestive enough for voluptuaries.

Oysters have their own sex lives, of course. American oysters begin life as males, then turn female. European oysters, being more decadent in such matters, flip flop back and forth in indecision. Both, like Tiresias, can be asked which gender enjoys sex more; like Lewis Carroll's oysters, however, they remain mute. Though indeed they have mouths, and stomachs, livers, hearts, kidneys, anuses, all of which we swallow when we devour them whole, just what is what within an oyster is hard to say. His sedentary life makes him fat and flabby;

in comparison, his relative the clam, adapted to burrowing, is muscular. The only chewy part of the oyster is the muscle with which he opens and closes his shell. It is this muscle which you must sever before he—or she—will slide off the shell and down your throat. His unhealthy couch potato—to mix kingdoms—life makes the oyster juicy, a watery delight whose salinity reveals how salty is his habitat.

Because oysters tolerate a wide range of waters, buying oysters is akin to buying wines; you need to know the provenance of both. Some vineyards tempt you with low-priced demijohns of rotgut; some oystermongers tempt you with gigantic oysters which, opened, are as bland as mush. Promoters in Charleston concocted the Lowcountry Oyster Festival to take a few more dollars from the unwary, and promised bushels of oysters. Which there were— from Florida, local oyster factories being unable to find enough oysters for such crowds. Not that it mattered; most of the people attending were no more native than the oysters, and couldn't tell a Bull's Bay oyster from a Floridian if it opened its shells and spit on them.

My father claimed he could. Bull's Bay oysters, he said, were smaller but saltier and sweeter than anything that came out of Chesapeake. Florida couldn't make an oyster worth opening, he opined. He had more than regional pride to back him up: Bull's Bay is far saltier than either Chesapeake or Apalichicola. Consequently, its oysters are saltier—smaller, growing in tidal clusters unlike the others' deep-water singles.

At one oyster roast we threw, Daddy became annoyed with an out-of-stater who maintained the superiority of Chesapeake oysters. Daddy maintained the visitor knew not whereof he spoke, that he couldn't tell the difference between local oysters much less interstate, but that he, Daddy, could and would deter-mine "by taste alone" the provenance of the oysters we were eating. This he proceeded to do, with raw ones, as he claimed roasting them added the taste of wood cut miles from the oyster's home. To assure honesty, he had the vis-itor select three oysters from three different sacks for Daddy's delectation. My father rinsed his hands as carefully as any surgeon in pre-op, not wanting to prejudice the flavor with juices from oysters from another creek. He held each oyster high, turning it round and round in his hand, nibbling the shell, "to taste the algae, you know," he told us. Taking an oyster knife he'd rinsed, he carefully pried one open, laid it down in its half shell, rinsed his hands and knife again, and did the same to the other two. Returning to the first, he lifted it in its shell, sniffed it, and sipped its liquor, turning it round and round in his mouth, then spit it out. He called for a jigger of Scotch "to clean my palate," and allowed as how he didn't need to eat the oyster to tell where it came from. "The creekwater gives it its flavor," he said. "Eating the oyster itself will just confuse my taste buds." His palate having been cleansed and re-cleansed, "just in case," he returned to his tasting.

"Well, these first two are obviously from Copahee. They've got a good salty bouquet with muddy undertones, and there ain't a muddier bay I know of. This last one, though, he's from the bottom reaches of Porcher's; he's got that good clean taste you get with a strong current and just a hint, barely enough to taste, of gasoline drifting in from the Waterway."

We were all mighty impressed, of course, but as someone observed, how the hell was anyone to tell if Daddy was right or wrong? "Call up Phil Porcher; he got them, didn't he? He'll know." So someone called Porcher, asked him where he'd taken his oysters from. Porcher told him, and damned if my father wasn't right. "Phil says he's been oystering in Copahee and the mouth of Porcher's."

That settled it, and Daddy remained oysterman extraordinaire the whole afternoon. He held the visitor to the bottle of Scotch they'd bet. After everyone had left, I asked him how he'd done it, and he swore to me that it was taste alone. Years later, though, when I'd reached my maturity (as he liked to say) we were eating oysters and the oyster-tasting came up. "What that jackass didn't know that I knew," Daddy confided, "was that Phil Porcher didn't oyster anywhere but in Copahee and Porcher's. All that nonsense about taste I just threw in to color things a bit."

Nowadays the government requires vendors to tag their oysters, stating where and when they were harvested—and such tags reveal much. Once I ordered from a local grocery store a bushel of Chesapeake oysters; they turned out to have been harvested in Apalachicola, Florida, two and a half weeks earlier. Even without a tag, you'd might have guessed they weren't Chesapeake; they were too big and bland. They'd come from some place with brackish waters, with a climate so warm oysters could grow nearly year round.

Chesapeake oysters were overharvested one hundred fifty years ago by New Englanders who, having exhausted their own beds, migrated southward, ravaging beds around Cape Cod, Long Island Sound, Staten Island, and Delaware Bay, arriving in the Chesapeake in the first two decades of the nineteenth century. Pollution and habitat destruction ruined what overzealous harvesting hadn't; with everyone along the East Coast flushing their toilets into the Chesapeake, it's a wonder there're any oysters left to eat, and that the ones left don't have suspicious undertones.

Ironically, pollution may save the oyster. Polluted beds, off-limits to humans, flourish while safe beds, few in number, shrink from our contact, denuded, few of the shells taken from them ever being returned. Every driveway, garden path and fake tabby facade installed permanently removes thousands of shells, every bushel you and I buy is a bushel less of shells for oyster sprat to settle on.

Wandering my home waters, I feel like that new-born oyster spat must when it realizes its home has been misappropriated by others and, though native, he is a stranger in a strange land doomed to die homeless.

8

Clams

Across the creek from Porcher's Bluff's dock, a ring of oyster beds encircles a sandy pool. Novelist Zane Grey never imagined a more beautifully hidden valley than this one, with fiddlers on the oyster cliffs semaphoring like hostile Indians planning an ambush one moment, stampeding like a herd of buffalo the next. My stepson Nicholas and I lie full-length in a pool as tepid as a bath; woodstorks ride in lazy circles the thermals bursting into white thunderheads above us. Resting on a thousand mud snails, I am nibbled by shrimp. Raking the sand mindlessly with my fingers, I encounter hard crescent shapes: we are in a clam bed.

Steeping in our salt stew, we have stumbled upon a trove of cherrystones. An untouched clam bed is a marvelous thing; your fingers encounter food wherever they alight and, blindly, you feel out whether tonight's meal is steamed clams or chowder. Sarah loves cherrystones, abhors larger chowder clams, whereas Nicholas, preferring size to taste, will eat nothing small. Between the two of them, we can clear the creek of clams, should we desire.

Daddy wisely forbade his children from clambering about on razor-sharp oyster beds. Instead, he encouraged us to play in the sandy stretches of creek and taught us how to feel with our feet for the lunar shapes of clams. Too young to throw even a child-sized cast net, we nevertheless felt important filling a bucket with the clams we "caught." Not for us the niceties of distinction among cherrystones, littlenecks, and chowders; we vied for who could find the most and the largest. Passing the skill on to Nicholas costs me—I must carry a bucket weighed down with clams enough for days of chowder—but his joy is the same I felt forty years ago, the thrill of harvesting your own meat. I know from experience he will never eat all the clams he has caught; I know, too, that to throw them back now is to dampen his delight. We will steam some of them tonight, steam more in tomorrow's bouillabaisse, and puree the rest for gumbo.

Few people on the Bluff eat clams on a regular basis; there are too many fish and shrimp and oysters. Our major rivals are clamcrackers—skates and rays—who scoop out holes in the sand bars with their wings looking for clams. After a school of skates has passed, the bars are cratered worse than the moon with their circular trace. Most craters do not exceed two feet in diameter, though every now and then a larger one reminds you there are beasts in the water you'd just as soon not meet alone; creatures such as the devilfish and manta ray can reach twenty-two feet in width and weigh over three thousand pounds.

Huge but harmless, devilfish occasionally visit our bays and sounds; one antebellum writer recounts the wild rides he took behind harpooned devilfish in Port Royal Sound, a hundred miles south of Porcher's. A colonial account would have you believe the devilfish "has been known to weigh a Sloop's Anchor, and run with the Vessel a League or two, and bring her back, against the Tide, to almost the same place." Pilots flying small planes low over shallow coastal waters report manta rays' Stealth bomber-shaped forms so huge they engulf whole the plane's shadow. Four feet's the largest wingspan I've measured in Porcher's, so I scarcely worry about such giants.

Stingrays, on the other hand, abound, and their sting can be painful. In 1608 Captain John Smith was one of the first Europeans to fall victim to the stingray, being stung by one he had impaled on his sword; ". . . no bloud or wound was seene, but a little blew spot, but the torment was instantly so extreame, that in foure houres had so swolen his hand, arme and shoulder, we all with much sorrow concluded his funerall, and prepared his grave in an Island by, as himselfe directed: yet it pleased God by a precious oyle Docter Russell at first applyed to it when he sounded it with probe (ere night) his tormenting paine was so well asswaged that he eate of the fish to his supper . . ."

Most Americans have not followed Smith's example, and it is difficult to find ray or skate on a seafood menu or in the store. Surf fishers routinely leave those they catch to die on the beach. Nevertheless, both skate and ray "wings" make good eating, though, like shark, they must be bled and gutted quickly to rid them of urea, which will ruin the taste. The wings, which are greatly enlarged pectoral fins—like the smaller ones you find behind a fish's gills— are filled with flattened, rib-like stays of cartilage, which skates, rays, and sharks use in lieu of bones. Skate wing tastes something like scallops; indeed, unscrupulous vendors use cookie cutters to manufacture "scallops" from skates' wings. Similarly, many a shark has been sold for swordfish steaks, if dockside tales are true.

Clamcrackers have been cracking Carolina clams for hundreds of thousands, perhaps millions, of years. Examine one you find dead on the beach, and you'll find a mouth with small, flattened teeth resembling miniature paving stones. Area rivers—the Ashley, Cooper, Edisto and Wando—are littered with identical fossil fragments of skate and ray teeth. Mingled with these are petrified mud casts of their dinners, clams and oysters. Many a time I've pulled a clam up from Porcher's bottom only to discover it dead and filled with mud. Likewise, these fossil clam casts were mud within a buried clam. The shell has long since worn away, leaving its imprint in stone, an imprint so perfect you can still make out surface details of the vanished shell; perfect, petrified cherrystones several million years too old to eat.

Marine fossils mingle with terrestrial on these beaches. Clams rub backs with prehistoric horses' teeth, which graze next to teeth dropped from forty–foot long sharks. Wood worn by water and worm floats beside petrified oysters, to whose ancient remains present-day oysters cling in a family connection that beggars the pedigrees of European nobility. The rivers have cut through several distinct strata, mingling fossils of various ages with the flotsam and jetsam of man, Indian pottery, trade goods like beads and pipes, Coke cans, and styrofoam cups, and everywhere are nodules of phosphate, irregularly rounded stones darkly colored brown and black, and shot through with holes and tunnels so perfect you think them manmade. They're natural, however, formed by chemical reaction when this land was seabed and the Alps and Himalayas but pubescent pimples on the face of the land. Two hundred miles offshore similar nodules are forming as you read, out on the Blake Plateau, an immense seaplain that ends in the eighteen-thousand-foot high Blake-Bahamas Scarp.

Lowcountry phosphate beds were once big business. An ad in an 1867 book proclaims, "The 'CAROLINA FERTILIZER' is made from the

PHOSPHATES of South Carolina, and is pronounced by various chemists one of the best Manures known, only inferior to Peruvian Guano in its FERTILIZING PROPERTIES. These PHOSPHATES are the remains of extinct land and sea animals, and possess qualities of the greatest value to the agriculturist. . . . We will furnish this excellent FERTILIZER to Planters and others at $65 per ton of 2000 pounds."

Accompanying this blurb is a picture of "extinct land and sea animals," an adaptation of a popular French engraving showing a spouting ichthyosaur and long-necked plesiosaurus in background combat while their skeletons lie foregrounded on a beach shaded by giant club mosses. As I understand evolution, this picture mingles Carboniferous land plants from three hundred twenty million years ago with warring monsters from the two-hundred-million-year-old Age of Dinosaurs in order to sell phosphates formed from five to thirty million years ago during the Age of Mammals. Advertisers, it seems, were no less bound to the truth a hundred years ago than they are today.

Porcher's is at least as much a jumble as this ad. Nicholas and I bathe in a clam bed whose inhabitants' names confuse while preserving European and Native American languages and uses. Clams have been called *clams* in English since at least 1500. Back then, a *clam* was a *clamp*, and *clam*shells clam or clamp together. What I call clams Sarah calls quahogs. That's because I grew up on a Southern seacoast and she, benighted landlubber, discovered my clams only when she moved to coastal New England where the settlers, copying the Narragansett Indians of Rhode Island, called the bivalves quahogs and, also copying the Indians, had clambakes on the beaches. Our southern beaches are sand, not stone, and so seaside clambakes never caught on down south. Scientists call my clam and Sarah's quahog *Venus mercenaria*, the species name *mercenaria* recalling that Indians used these shells to make *wampum* or *wampumpeag*, large beaded cloths made from cylindrical beads of clamshell. In English, *wampum* now means money, but to the Algonquin Indians whose word it is, wampum meant "white string." Algonquin white strings were not only used for money, but also for ornament and as a form of communication, the various patterns woven from the purple and white beads telling stories to those who knew their language. I have seen wampum belts only in France, where Rouen Cathedral had on display in its museum large vestments and altar cloths made of wampum. Mute though beautiful stories decorate the beaded cloths, stories neither I nor the curators could read.

Porcher's bluffs narrate a tale in shell I only recently learned to read. The Bluff itself derives its name from shell-capped bluffs that line both sides of the creek where it first reaches high land. These bluffs were the first "stone" I knew, my childhood playland being largely sand and clay. Like sedimentary strata in a gorge, Porcher's blue-grey bluffs read vertically from top to bottom. The story they tell of that civilization gone with the wind is not Margaret Mitchell's, however. It is more akin to agribusiness than to gracious living. Year after year of cotton exhausted Carolina's fields; prices were good and he was a fool who let land lie fallow. So depleted did the land become that many had to leave it, going west to Texas, where a South Carolinian, William Travis, would command the desperate American stand at the Alamo in 1836. Those who farmed the land around Porcher's were luckier; they had the sea to help them, and there they sent their slaves for the oysters with which to lime their fields.

Like the vanished Indians before them, they set out at half-tide, floating downcreek with the current to where the banks were lined with dead shell. Six muddy hours later they returned, scows riding low in the water, a hundred thousand shells a scow. They heaped shell on the banks near the cotton fields, and burned it down in huge bonfires to make lime to fertilize the fields. If you are patient enough, you can read the record of fire upon fire, each having left a thin layer of solidified shell upon which the next was laid.

Imagine how many oysters, how many trees, each bonfire consumed. In those long-gone days who would have ever thought we could cut down an entire continent of trees? Who would have thought we'd eat so many oysters, take away so many shells that oystering would die out along most of the East Coast? Who but a prophetic few would have thought we'd fight the bloodiest war in our history to free the slaves whipped into the forests to timber and the marshes to harvest shell? Certainly, the Porcher's didn't. Porcher's Bluff as a name on the land dates only from 1859, two years before the Civil War, when the Porchers built the big old house that's still there. Such is not the work of people who think their cause a dying one.

The shell bluffs along Porcher grew no more after 1865. Slavery was over, the planters bankrupted, and phosphate mining only two years away. Today they stand mute witness to a moment in the creek's history, the work of one generation who left forever their mark upon the land. You can see the bluffs from the sea islands three miles away, the only stone bluffs along that part of the coast. This has given rise to the supposition that they are where the pirates buried the treasure in Poe's "Goldbug," set on nearby Sullivan's Island.

Perhaps, perhaps not. Poe enthusiasts have also found in a Charleston graveyard the grave of one A.L., purported model for Poe's Annabel Lee. My father, ignoring the fact that Poe was an entirely unknown private when he was stationed on Sullivan's Island, claimed "he'd take the ferry over from Mt. Pleasant to the city where he dined with some of Charleston's finest." He could also point out to you fictional Rhett Butler's ancestral home where, he said, Margaret Mitchell attended a debutante ball. My mother claimed my daddy, although a newspaperman, never let the facts stand in the way of a good story.

He told me more than once of the pirate ship that anchored off Dewee's Inlet in front of Porcher's Creek. We'd be sitting on the front porch, rocking and drinking, me beer, him Scotch. "Sometime in 1716, I forget the month, the Charleston *Gazette* reported two ships' captains a week apart both told of seeing a pirate ship anchored off Dewee's." Raising his glass, Daddy would point down the creek and continue, "Three miles thataway. That was two years before Blackbeard's death, two years before they hung Stede Bonnet for a pirate in Charleston, and buried his body in the marsh. You know that story, don't you?" Off we'd go down a rabbit hole for ten minutes before returning to Dewee's. "What would a pirate be doing anchored offshore for a week? Waiting for a careless ship? Restocking water and meat? Maybe. But maybe he was burying his treasure. Anyway, Poe would have heard stories of these pirates when he dined in town, when he stood where Bonnet hung. During the long hours on guard duty at Fort Moultrie, he could have looked north to the white cliffs of Porcher's, and embroidered what he'd heard in town of pirates and their treasure."

"Maybe" became "for certain" over the years. The pirates became conquistadors. Legends of visiting Spaniards have been handed down for generations along the coast. History confirms their presence. Cape Romain was named by the Spanish, and an early map notes "Hispanis" in the vicinity of "Capo romano." Bull Island to the south of Cape Romain hides a harbor on its northern end, a forty-foot-deep harbor with a good flow of fresh water. Spanish, French and English explorers used to anchor here. Here the English first planned to build Charleston, and here the Spanish and French landed in an ill-fated invasion attempt. Here also the English built a fort to guard against French and Spanish marauders and pirates of all nationalities.

As a child, my father heard these stories. He grew up on a plantation situated atop an Indian mound on Awendaw Creek, landward of Bull Island and Cape Romain and north of Porcher's. Who knows, he and his family surmised, might not a Spanish treasure fleet, driven off course by one hell of a hurricane, have tried to outrun the storm, hoping to make landfall at Bull Island, behind whose northern tip they could shelter? Surfing landward on a storm surge, did they miss the tip and rip their bottoms out somewhere in the marsh off Awendaw?

Perhaps the crew, Daddy would posit to me, the ones who survived, enslaved the local Indians, had them build a palisade fort outside the Indian village proper, and then salvaged the ship. Perhaps they buried the doubloons and pieces of eight in the middle of the palisade, right under the firehole, to hide any trace of them. Then they set to waiting for a passing ship to rescue them, waited and waited, but nobody came. Time passed until their hosts, fed up, massacred them, piled up everything Spanish into fire hole, and set it afire. Never found the gold; didn't even know it was there.

It's still there. If a body knew where to look, he'd be rich. Daddy's family looked for years. Dug up the lawn, bored exploratory holes up and down the creek bank, even dowsed for doubloons. All they found were oyster shells, horseshoes, and tin cans. His sister once found a perfect, unbroken pot, filled with periwinkles (that's now in the local museum), but no gold, no pieces of eight.

If one crew survived to salvage their gold, perhaps others died with it in the marsh. Government maps locate two known wrecks in Bull's Bay, coasters that went down a hundred years ago. My father knows of others not on the map. Seaward of White Banks, cobblestones litter the bay's floor, ballast from an unrecorded wreck. The ten miles of marsh behind Bull's Bay from Ghost Point to Moore's Landing could be hiding right now galleons and their treasure troves.

The mud can be several feet thick in the Bay. Daddy had a metal prod made, twenty feet long. We were going to sound the mud for gold. Divide the marsh into quadrants and pry out its secrets, one stab at a time.

Only trouble is, the marsh is government land. Used to be ours, Daddy says, but the government stole it back when he was a kid. So we'd have to sneak out there on the right tide, a full moon tide so as to get a boat up into that marsh. He figured we'd get two or three good days a month. We'd have to be on the lookout for wardens in boats and planes. They're always patrolling the place, up and down, in and out, looking for violators of regulations you didn't even know were on the books. Some you did, but chose to ignore. Once they caught our cousin smuggling marijuana in on a shrimp boat. You'd think from all the hullabaloo the Feds made over the case they'd caught a Colombian drug lord instead of a shrimper with a sideline. They took his boat, locked him up, and scared the hell out of everybody for a year or two.

To avoid the warden, Dad planned to hunt doubloons during the day. There's no law says you can't poke holes in mud if you want to. Once we found it, we'd come back at night and smuggle it out; hide it good, maybe bury it on my sister's land; and then rediscover it, legally, and retire.

One month it rained, the next the winds were wrong, the next month we couldn't get a boat. On and on it went until the gleam in Dad's eye waned, and he began scheming other get-rich-quick scams in the long dull days he passes, a mind marooned by age inside a dying body. We've still got that twenty-foot rod stored out in my sister's shed, just in case.

The only sunken boat in Porcher's is an oyster scow that sank midcreek a quarter of a mile upstream from where the dock runs six hundred feet across marsh and mud in search of the channel. That channel used to cut in close to land, right off the clump of four palmettos the Porchers planted a hundred years ago. You can still make out its former course in a slough that's knee-deep in mud at low tide. The Porchers made a bad mistake when they left the scow where it sank and poled around it. Over the years, the creek, its course blocked by the scow, has turned to port, cutting into the marsh and away from the Bluff. It now flows one hundred feet east of where it once flowed, an expensive one hundred feet when it came time to build a dock to deep water.

The creek giveth, and the creek taketh away. Where the main channel turns marshward, the bank erodes several feet a year. The marsh grows on a peaty mat of old marsh roots two feet thick in places. Beneath this peat is more easily eroded sand. Large chunks of peat collapse after storms into the creekbed, exposing more and more sand. This sand, three feet under water in today's high tides, was land four thousand years ago. You can still see the old tree roots, oak and pine and cedar, where the peat has preserved them. The rising sea flooded the forest, marsh replaced tree, and for four thousand years lay down peat at the rate of little over an inch a century. Fiddler crabs tunnel the peat and, at low tide, water streams out of their holes as from a sieve.

Where fiddlers fiddle today, Indians once strode: you find their traces nearly every time you go out. Floating the bank, I gather arrowheads and pottery shards decorated with dots and lines and holes and lunettes and checkerboards, hand-held stone axe-heads and flint-scrapers. So much that, at times, you suspect these former Americans of having been as careless with their belongings as we are with our beer cans and plastic bags. "Made in China," "Fabrique en France," "Made in Milwaukee": our litter proclaims our trade routes. So too does the Indians', these stones that erode out of Porcher's banks having come from mountains far inland. They traveled by foot, Indian traders, carrying their ware two or three hundred miles in buckskin bags on their backs. What worth did a pound of stone fragments take as it wore into weary backs?

Did wampum made of Porcher's clams go inland in exchange? Do Porcher's beads, having followed trails alongside the rivers, lie buried at the foot of mountains? Might not a belt of Porcher wampum have been traded from tribe to tribe, making its way west to California, north to Canada? Might not these exiled belts, telling perhaps the story of their southern origin in patterns no longer understood, have been woven into wampumpeag and given to the black-robed priests of Christ who, in turn, took them home to France? Might not the very wampumpeag altar cloths I vainly tried to read in Rouen have been greeting me, if only I spoke their tongue, with tales of Porcher's from long, long ago? Perhaps they do; certainly, it is no more foolish a fancy than that of pirates or conquistadores.

9

Mullet

I am a mullet. Or so an administrator where I work has labeled me. Useless, he means, revealing himself to know nothing, of mullet at least. Only a land-lubber of the soul or palate would think mullet a "trash" fish.

To dislike mullet is to admit that you buy your fish instead of catching it. Fresh mullet is a delight unmatched by any other fish in the creek. Unlike flounder and other white fish which taste like so much raw dough unless they borrow flavor from spices or sauces, mullet tastes of the creek itself. Muddy, the unappreciative claim; but these are people who pay others to do their fish-ing for them. I say to them that they too would smell no sweeter than a day's old mullet were they not to bathe upon leaving the creek.

Nothing stinks like old creek clothes. Leave them unrinsed and piled in the corner of your porch or bathroom, and you will smell them out tomorrow. Life so chokes Porcher's summer waters that she runs grey with it; hold a glass up to the light and you will see a thousand minute lives floating oblivious of you and your self-importance. Look at these under a lens or microscope: hatchet-headed, bug-eyed, clawed, fingered, fanned, horned, helmeted, seg-mented, globular, serpentine, floating, pulsating, swimming, grazing, siphon-ing, hunter and hunted, a thousand unimaginable monsters, precursors of crab and shrimp and Darwin only knows what all else, parade before your aston-ished eyes. These are what flavor your forgotten creek clothes and mullet, who filter algae and plankton from the mud.

Cooked mullet are rich with hints of creek and sea and a just-enough-of-a-whiff-of-pluff mud to make me homesick even when I'm eating only thirty yards from the creek itself. Fried mullet or boiled shrimp accompanied our hominy grits summer mornings when one of us had been lucky with the net. So oily a fish is mullet that you can sauté it in the pan by itself. I've been served flounder so dry I couldn't choke them down, but mullet is always moist, flaking off the bone and melting in my mouth. Mullet can be dressed up for dinner, baked with white wine and vegetables. Like most things from the creek, though, it is best cooked by itself, as it comes from the creek.

Whenever I catch mullet, I shed years, returning to my childhood and the joy of successful fishing, of feeling a net jerk with two or three fish worth keeping. Nothing hooks someone on the creek like fishing for mullet. I seduced my stepsons and their mother with mullet, as my father had seduced me with them. Mullet and shrimp divide the creek's holes between them, fish favoring these, shrimp those holes. The only way to tell which hole is which is to cast nets into them all; a shrimp hole may harbor a few mullet, but a mullet hole seldom if ever harbors shrimp.

Porcher's sand flats hide low tide holes choked with mullet. "Stand here," I told my ten-year-old stepson Chris, "and wait until I tell you to cast." I then walked round the bank of a twenty-five-foot-long hole and began wading back towards him. The water rippled, then whitened, where mullet broke the surface; as I scared them farther, they leapt out of the water. "Now," I shouted, and Chris heaved his net into the living water. "Tuck it up, tuck it up," I told him, joining him on the bank. "I've caught something! I've caught something!" he shouted as he pulled in on the line and the net heaved and tugged back at him. "Pull him on in, pull him on in!" I said, "and walk him back up the bank." Chris dragged his net out and onto the sand; two mullet, each nearly eighteen inches long, writhed in the pursed mesh. "Mummy, come look, come look! I've caught two fish!"

The creek had caught Chris, as it had me forty years before.

Mullet were lessons in anatomy, since "clean what you catch" was house rule number one. Mullet die quickly out of water, and most were hardening in rigor mortis by the time I'd reach the dock. Some would yet be living, however, and these provided crude lessons in torture and murder. I'd imagine what it felt like, being scaled while yet alive, shitting upon a knife tip inserted into my anus, bleeding to death as a serrated knife hacked through my neck and spinal column. I'd move from victim to victim, using the same slime-fouled spoon to scale them all, the same reeking knife to decapitate them, rinsing the living and dead in the same bloody bucket. I was a Robespierre of the creek, chop, chop, chopping my way through the mullet aristocracy, a teenage Aztec, practicing barbaric rituals upon fish, a serial killer in training, a surgeon in the rough.

More careful cutting reveals the hidden beauty of inner organs nestled each against the other: the rich reds of heart and liver; the grey-green coils of full intestines; the pale pink of empty intestines; and, every so often, the brilliant yellow sausages of roe fretted with blue and red blood vessels.

How strange that such beauty requires death to manifest itself. Like Macbeth, I wonder, "Will all great Neptune's ocean wash this blood/ Clean from my hand? No; this my hand will rather/ The multitudinous seas incarnadine,/ Making the green one red?" Would that I had a mullet god to whom I might pray for forgiveness. My god, of course, has no truck with such thoughts; after all, it was he who helped the disciples catch and eat all those fish in John's Gospel.

I keep a tally for the god of mullet should he want a count of my murders. Fish eyes, when baked, harden into light, meringue-like pearls. I store these in a jar: "Those are pearls that were his eyes:/ Nothing of him that doth fade,/ But doth suffer a sea-change/ Into something rich and strange."

Like baked mullet eyes, my father's eyes grow grey and cloudy. He watched his father's world grow dim and disappear under cataracts. Now his fades far away as I look on through glasses I have taken recently to wearing. When I held my grandfather's gnarled hand in my youthful one and led him to the dinner table for a meal of mullet, I did not foresee what I see now, my own hand, grown veiny and old, steadying my infant son's unlined hand dwarfed in my father's claw.

"This boy had mullet yet?" my father asked on a recent visit, already knowing the answer. "Goddamn it, get him out in the creek and baptize his ass. And be sure you bring me back some mullet."

We feasted that evening on hominy grits and sliced tomatoes and fresh mullet. Edward, his fingernails dark with pluff mud, ate his first meat—mullet. He liked it.

10

Blue Crabs

We all feel at times like Eliot's Prufrock, who thought himself a "pair of ragged claws scuttling across the floors of silent seas." It is well to remember, in such self-pitying moments, the blue crab. An ill-tempered, ornery son-of-a-bitch, so perfectly camouflaged you'd step on him before you saw him, except that he'll see you long before you see him, and scuttle off to deep water.

We used to search the holes for crabs at low tide. Most holes shallow enough to wade will have one or more crabs in them. Daddy taught us how to step on them, pinning their claws down, and then how to reach behind and pick them up by their hind legs. That way, they can't reach round and pinch the hell out of you. Anyone ever pinched by a blue crab knows they can draw blood if they're so inclined. The last thing Daddy wanted in the creek with him was caterwauling children.

Caught, the crabs would splay out their arms and legs, making themselves into weapons for us to chase each other with until Daddy intervened. "Don't torture the poor bastards. Put them in the bucket and find some more." So we'd scour the creek bed for crabs. Cornered, a blue crab raises itself bowlegged on its eight legs, claws up and open before it, in a stance guaranteed to frighten the small fish and crabs it preys on, and bellicose enough to give pause to a five-year-old. Captured, a blue can be easily subdued; turn him over, rub his belly, and he'll go to sleep.

Magnificent animals, blue crabs have the rakish lines of a predator. Their tapered sides and compressed shells suggest an alien spacecraft whose intergalactic reaches are the sea; their armor of jagged edges, lethal spines and vicious, blood-drawing claws that they have not come in peace. Blue crabs' superbly camouflaged olive green backs the color of creek mud give way to brilliant white bellies in newly molted specimens; so white you think it should be soft, but it's hard, lean and mean, and mottles with age as if it were rusting. A male blue's underarms—from which the species gets its common name—are deep, brilliant winter sky blue. Both male and female have red tipped claws, the female's being more obviously red because, it's said, she paints her fingernails.

We could always scare up single crabs in shallow tidal pools, but what we sought were doubles, a male and a female mating. A mating male hesitates before leaving his female, which means we stood a better chance of catching him than randier singles quick to scuttle away. Mating males often have a good size to them; they're "keepers," worth the trouble of boiling and picking.

The female is liable to be a "softie," as William Warner explains in *Beautiful Swimmers*, his Pulitzer Prize-winning history of the Chesapeake Bay crab industry. He reports that female blues copulate only when soft-shelled. A male locates a willing female and "cradles" her, sheltering her between his legs while she undergoes her final molt. Casting off her shell, she's soft for two to three days. Absolutely soft the first half day or so, crunchy but edible for about a day, hard-shelled as an ex-wife after three days. Commercial crabbers can tell how close to molting a cradled female is by looking at her see-through, flattened swimming leg. As kids, though, we'd feel her. If she was hard, she went into the bucket with the other crabs. If she was soft, we killed her, to keep her from hardening up. Come supper, we'd fry her up and eat her, shell and all.

Holding a soft shell was a good lesson in just what an exoskeleton's all about. She'd be so soft she'd flop like a rag doll, so soft she couldn't even hold up her claws, much less bite with them. Her hard-shelled mate, on the other hand, would be circling the bottom of the bucket on his tiptoes, claws raised and snapping. Killing soft-shells is intimate work; holding the soft-shell in one hand, we'd stick our other hand's thumb into her face, which collapsed, and gouge our way through what brain she had, and back out. She'd quiver and die. Then we'd peel back her shell, scoop out her greenish "fat" and scrape out the "dead man's fingers," sickly white "fingers" that are, in fact, gills but which were, according to our father, kidneys, one bite of which could kill you. Rinse her out in the creek from which we'd pulled her, and place her safe in the bucket, under a blanket of shrimp.

Everyone disliked the intimacy of killing softies. There's less connection when boiling water does the job for you. Daddy used to boil the crabs. We actually enjoyed the moment when he'd dump them in the big pot reserved for them. The crabs would clack and clatter with frantic activity, an occasional one letting out a "scream," a high-pitched squeal of what we took to be pain, and then grow quiet.

If we wanted a mess of crabs, we'd use a crab pot, a squat cage, two feet long and wide, a tad shorter in height. The frame's made of rebar—the metal bars used in reinforced concrete—and what looks like chicken wire, expensive chicken wire, having been treated with zinc in order not to rust. The pot itself is divided into lower and upper halves, an entry and a parlor. The entry's baited with frozen fish heads; heads are harder to pick apart than other offal, and frozen heads are easier to stuff in the cylindrical bait box. Crabs smell out the bait and crawl through funnel-like openings called throats [throats, entries and parlors—crabbers never heard of mixed metaphors]. Unable to reach the bait, their natural tendency is to escape through narrow passages upwards into the parlor. Once ensconced, they politely wait to be harvested. A parlor filled with blue crabs is a nicer place than many a human parlor I've been privy to.

They're called pots because their English ancestors were, in fact, pot-shaped wicker baskets. New England's lobster pots were the first American cousins of English crab pots. Blue crab pots are but the latest branch of the family, invented by a Chesapeake Bay waterman back before World War II. My father remembers, before pots came into Carolina, crabbers ran trot lines, teasing crabs netward with infinite skill and patience. Today's pots are tied to a rope which is tied to a buoy, often as not a plastic bleach or milk bottle. Weighted with rebar, the pot sinks to the bottom, a passive trap waiting for passing crabs. Commercial crabbers have a motorized pulley on their gunwales; they hook the rope in it and whir, whir, whir, the boat does all the work. Hauling in by hand a seaweed coated rope is a wet and cold task in January and February.

State residents are allowed two pots each before they're considered commercial and need a license. Although, with eight people in our house, we were entitled to sixteen pots, we seldom had more than two or three. Fifteen, twenty, maybe thirty crabs a pot meant we didn't need to avail ourselves of all our legal limits. We depended upon chance, anyway, for our pots. Weekend boaters run down their fair share of crabpot buoys, cutting the rope and so condemning whatever crabs are caught to cannibalism until only one, well-fed crab remains and he dies of starvation, caught in a crabpot lost in the bottom of a hole. Northeasters will flush such forgotten pots out of holes, casting them up on mud flats and marshbanks. Commercial crabbers have little use for these battered, rusting relics, but we did, hauling them home, cleaning them up and using them for another season or two until they fell apart.

We were careful only to take long-lost pots. Crabpot robbing is not done lightly in Carolina. Daddy claimed more than one robber's boat has been found drifting, its skipper's weighted legs feeding crabs in a secret creek hole. He'd tell us the story of a crabber missing for a week. Nobody knew where he'd gone. Crabbing on the creek was good, though, and everyone was out evenings with their chicken necks and crab nets. Crab casserole, crab cakes, crab soup, crab salad, and plain old crab filled everyone's plate that week. Then someone walked up the creek at low tide and came across what was left of a body. The crabs had been working on it for several days, drifting seaward when they'd had their fill. No one ate crab the rest of that summer, Daddy says.

We never found any such bodies in Porcher's, though she provided us year round with crabs. In the cool of the evening, we'd sit on the screened porch and pick them. Mother detested the tedium of crab picking, but it was one of the few times she shared with us. Crab-picking calls for a breeze. Even with a screen, no-see-'ums smelled us out and gathered round our eyes and mouths. After a few minutes of rubbing them, we'd be driven, screaming, into the creek to wash them and crab juice off. Meanwhile, the grownups calmed themselves with beer and bullshit.

Crab picking is a good time for bullshitting. It's a sloppy way to eat, newspaper spread over a picnic table, buckets of boiled crab, buckets of wash down water, and buckets of crab shells and offal. I remember as a kid sitting beside my father, learning how to pick crab or shrimp or shuck oysters, looking up with pride at him, listening to him swap tall and then taller tales with his friends. I was proud to be with the men, proud and a little apprehensive, wondering if they all knew how I was faking it sitting there pretending to be one of the guys, all the while trying to figure out how to became one of the guys. In a few years, it'll be my son's turn; I hope I'm man enough by then to let him in the secret: we're all faking it, walking creeks we've never seen before, fishing holes we're too scared to fathom. So eat up, son, and sneak a sip of my beer when I'm not looking.

Mostly what we catch in Porcher's are males. Females seem to prefer saltier water; shrimp boats come back with their decks filled with female crabs, most of them bearing orange sponges under their aprons—their eggs. By law, you have to throw back a she crab showing sponge. Not everyone does, since crab roe is the basis for she crab soup, a dish just this side of heaven.

She Crab Soup

at least a pound of lump crab meat and roe
4 tablespoons butter
1 teaspoon grated lemon rind
2 cups half and half cream
1 teaspoon Worcestershire sauce
mace, pepper and salt to taste
dry sherry to taste [at least four tablespoons]

Melt the butter in a heavy saucepan; stir in half-and-half, crab meat and roe, Worcestershire sauce, and seasonings; simmer ten to fifteen minutes. Remove from heat and add sherry. Serve hot.

Supposedly a Charleston specialty, she crab soup's popular in tourist restaurants. Much of what passes for she crab is, in fact, hard boiled egg soup, the crumbled up yolk providing both the texture and color of crab roe. Caveat emptor; even in death, a blue crab's liable to get the better of the unwary.

11

Escaping

Would that I had never left home. Driven by wanderlust and sure that I was fated to do great deeds, I fled Carolina happily. Though no Ancient Mariner, I have been here and there, seen a dozen other lands, crisscrossed my own in search of something I misplaced long ago.

Charleston first seduced me. Until I went off to college, I assumed all towns to be like mine, filled with old houses and narrow streets where one could walk for hours, daydreaming and observing, spending nothing but time. Who needed lunch in those carefree days when the walls and streets dripped food? I remember plucking red-orange pomegranates hanging over the walls of secret gardens, splitting them open to nibble the pulp from off their red, winking wet seeds, little guessing that each seed I stole condemned me to a year in exile.

Behind the funeral home was a yard choked on banana trees growing higgledy-piggledy from an earth we boys knew to be fecund with body parts. Leaves longer than our growing bodies hid obscenely swollen purple-headed flowers arcing down from their green girdle of leaves like the engorged phalli of horses or dogs. Thick with flies, the flowers shed petal after petal, growing ever farther out on their stalks, and sprouted miniature bananas, sweet, red-fleshed halflings just the size for a stolen snack.

In March the loquat ripened, yellowy-orange and sweet and hanging over every other wall in town. No one but boys ate them, and each of us had "his" tree in which he'd sit and gorge. Often as not these trees were in someone else's yard, but private property meant little to us then, when the brick walls separating yards were highways to adventure. We'd take off from my cousin Henry's backyard, running along our four-inch-wide sidewalks, six feet in the air, intimate with each loose brick, each laundry line strung with strange female garments, each barking dog, passing yards adorned with swimming pools and croquet sets, past a yard choked with a bamboo forest in whose jungle depths we hunted cats and birds and one another, past a scuppernong arbor so thickly tangled that only we divined the secret rooms festooned with grapes free for the picking, to a formal garden gone to seed behind walls lined with broken bottle tops. Here we wandered moss-grown alleys shaded by loquats gone rampant, rinsed our faces in a goldfish pond rank with cattails, and foraged forgotten treasures in moldering outbuildings. Always with a weathered eye to the begrimed windows of the hulking mansion, from whose depths a withered Mrs. Havisham might any moment emerge, loosing her black mastiff on "you goddamned ragamuffins." We would scatter, running for the nearest wall and, broken bottles be damned, up through a tree's branches and onto our precarious perches, Cerberus' breath behind us, pockets filled with loquats all the sweeter for being stolen.

We knew each family's weekly schedule better than they did, when Mary fried chicken and Emma broiled fish and Louisa made red rice. We'd show up ten minutes before dinner, just in time for someone's mother to invite us to stay, and to yell back to the kitchen to "set an extra plate." Dinner was served in formal dining rooms, cool caverns shuttered against the heat and light out-doors, sideboards groaning with ancestral china patterns, and heavy sterling forks and knives glinting in candlelight. Emma, Louisa, or Mary—wearing always the same white apron and black dress—carried course after wonder-ful course into us from the kitchen through swinging doors. There was pear chutney, artichoke relish, pickled watermelon rinds, figs, shrimp and tomatoes smiled up from glass dishes; brown, red, white, yellow, pilaud, casseroled, steamed, boiled, fried, baked, hot, cold, sour, sweet, main course, side course, dessert, and always rice, bowl upon bowl of rice; and pitchers of dark, almost-black ice tea to wash it down with, sweet and minty tepid teas whose secret recipes disappeared when the women who made them died or retired.

My garden in Virginia chokes on mints I've grown from sprigs stolen or begged from a dozen Charleston homes, mints whose great-great-great-great-great grandsprigs are said to have shipped west from England three hundred years ago bound for the New World, whose colonial descendant leaves are said to have freshened the breaths of George Washington, Lafayette, and Cornwallis, whose later scions flavored mouths that kissed Confederate Beauregard goodbye. Today I buy myself designer teas, oolongs and Dhargheelings flavored with bergamot and whatnot. When homesickness for my youth steals over me, for that time when the world was fresh and full of promise, I abjure these arriviste pretenders and brew myself a blacker-than-sin pan of Lipton and mint and sugar enough to turn me diabetic. For a moment, I can fool myself, pretend that I am sitting on a veranda overlooking Charleston harbor, that the wind is in the palmettos, and the steeple bells are ringing.

My yard is a failed oasis for Caroliniana. Like a college co-ed who takes her stuffed bears with her, I lugged up north bananas, camellias, gardenias, ginger lilies, crepe myrtles, live oaks, cassina, wax myrtles, oleanders—whatever I could dig up in my sister's woods and yard that reminded me of long ago and far away.

My house in winter becomes a refuge for sun-starved, freeze-fearing, potted prisoners. I, their warden, chain myself to them, watering, misting, nursing them from first frost in September through last in May, watching them grow spindly and pale, moving them from plant-choked window to plant-choked window, following the sun in its southern retreat and slow, oh-how-so-slow return.

For five years I nurtured my banana, who steadfastly refused to grow more than two feet high, and even more firmly refused to bloom. Gardenias came and went without those rich, white blooms whose perfume takes me back to high school proms, slow waltzes and crushed corsages. Branches from oleanders under whose shade we sat as children grew sickly long and longer, bending this way and that in the window like trapped serpents. From little acorns live oaks grew, too tall for pots, too spindly to look at with anything but pity.

Those that I planted outdoors fared even worse. Freed from the lush competition of Porcher's woods, my transplants flourished in the summer only to huddle under haybales in winter, life sapping from them freeze by freeze. Come spring, I'd turn under the brittle carcasses of crepe, cassina and myrtle and try again to resurrect the past.

Not that I am the first to try in vain to relive his youth. I once knew a man from the Eastern Shore of Virginia who'd had the misfortune to move inland. Once a year he made the trek back, taking his children in the vain hope that they too would call this tidal land home. Vacation over, he'd carry a bushel basket of live blue crabs westward strapped to his car's rooftop. Four hours he'd drive, baptizing with salt water and crab spittle the Tidewater, the Piedmont, the Blue Ridge, the Valley of Virginia. Like him, his crabs withered so far from home, and we'd sniff him out the morrow morn, his garbage stuffed with crabs who died homesick for the Chesapeake.

As a child, my brother Timothy took pity on the homeless blue crabs that came in as part of our catch. Daddy invariably found crabs and fish too small to keep mixed in with the shrimp and mullet. These he unceremoniously dumped on the lawn, to the delight of our dogs, who gobbled gasping fish and teased nipping crabs to death. My brother snuck the crabs into our freshwater pond. Where they lived—for a while.

None lived to shed a shell or reproduce; they could not survive translation from salt to fresh. My coastal plants die like those crabs when I bring them inland. I, however, have survived my translation from salt to freshwater creeks, have managed even to reproduce. The price is that for my children Porcher's will be a place to visit on vacation, a source of more happy than sad memories perhaps, but not home. Mine is the last generation of three centuries of Lelands to call this place home.

Today the Shenandoah amazes me with its beauty. The fall sky is that deep blue that seems to put within fingers' reach the mountains; when outer space itself is just beyond my grasp. The maples are flecked red and orange and green; the purple asters and goldenrod riot alongside the dirt roads Sarah and I hike, scaring up deer and woodchuck. A tree I thought a maple takes flight before us as a hundred Monarch butterflies fly up and away, heading south for the winter. Truly, this land is more beautiful than that of my childhood, and yet, and yet . . . I cannot shake the foreboding that, like my brother's crabs, though I am in sweeter water, I cannot shed my shell and grow.

12

Mosquito Ditches

In a dozen unheralded, unnamed bogs Porcher's begins. Unlike the Mississippi, no signpost announces, "Here begins Porcher's Creek." Uncelebrated, unremarked, its headwaters are more and more bulldozed, channeled, ignored, rerouted, remade, eradicated. What the government has not declared of value is of no value in Carolina.

Sarah complains that everything is flat and straight in the Lowcountry. I tell her she is wrong. Granted, we do not have the vertical relief the Shenandoah enjoys, but elevations vary, and nothing but man-made objects stay straight for long—which is how you know Porcher's headwaters have been altered.

Creeks snake, ditches run—an easy guide to determining whether what you stand before is natural or man-made. Porcher's in its beginnings runs through the woods as straight as the bottom line in an accountant's ledger. For farmers the land abutting Porcher's was neither wet enough for rice nor dry enough for cotton. The government later viewed Porcher's wetlands as merely mosquito breeding factories and tried to shut them down. Today developers also wish to change the creek's topography. All three hit upon the same solution: draining the wetlands.

Cypress and tupelo and maple and birch rise above a tangle of dwarf palmetto, smilax, and jessamine that was once fields, open to the sky. It would take a whip to get most folk today to enter the jungle that has reclaimed these fields. Two hundred and fifty years ago, whips drove black slaves into these antediluvian swamps of cattail and rush and moccasin, pickerel weed, willow and alligator, chopping trees, hauling stumps, cutting ditches.

Flying into Charleston you can spot these relic fields from the air. Cross the Santee Delta and you will see rice fields returning to swamp, and canal after canal running arrow-straight towards the horizon. Though they began as bogs, Porcher's fields, too high and dry for rice, grew cotton. Her slave-dug ditches still stitch the land, still draining swamp into marsh, although no one has planted crops or tended the ditches in fifty to a hundred years. Live oaks rise from these ditches' crumbling banks, their trunks two to three feet thick. Walking the marsh edge, I once came upon one such green tunnel, its mouth a flotsam-jammed morass of driftwood logs and oily rust-orange water floating on a foot of black, stinking mud. Fighting my way back through time and a hundred criss-crossed, hurricane-toppled pines gone gray with salt and sun, I reached a section that might have been a park, a grassy sward shaded by oaks whose gnarled branches, draped with green bracelets of resurrection fern and old man's beard, dipped low as if inviting climbers into their moss hung heights in which invisible warblers sang. Yet farther inland, shaded by oaks older than the first whites and blacks to settle here, was an Indian village slowly returning to the soil out of which it had arisen four, five, six thousand years ago. Perhaps an acre in extent, it was a landbound larger copy of those islands I knew from the marsh, its presence here dictated by the boggy spring which was the explanation for the ditch I had followed inland.

Summer evenings along Porcher's were filled with the sound of a thousand frogs from half a dozen different species croaking, bellowing, and peeping. Stridulating crickets, grasshoppers, cicadas, and katydids followed separate scores in a cacophonous, directorless symphony of strings. Away off in the night whippoorwills demanded justice, and Chuckwill's widows began their nightly plaint; night herons croaked, answered by the crazed cackles of marsh hens. The lulls that fell periodically betrayed the phhlfft-phhlfft of winged night creatures passing just out of sight overhead. Frantic bats flitted across the rising moon's face, a thousand fireflies mimicked the night sky and danced like Christmas lights in the shadows under the live oaks. Porch lights attracted hordes of nameless night bugs, hard-shelled orange and black and brown beetles that threw themselves loudly against the screens. Horned and pincered and jawed and toothed predators followed these, and around them all hovered small, nondescript grey and brown and white moths, among whom flew from time to time angelic luna moths. Were I to walk out at night, I'd crunch palmetto bugs and brush away those that flew towards me from the dark.

Spider's webs caressed my face. Under all this, like a basso obstinato, blood-seeking mosquitoes whined incessantly, joined by the hum of a thousand gnats and midges sheltering in my lee.

Mosquitoes explain the newer ditches lacing the woods around Porcher's; cedar, cherry, and sweet gum line these ditches dug by mosquito control programs after World War II. Two miles away from Porcher's proper, choked with whatever wouldn't fit in a garbage can—freezers, dryers, sofas, chairs—ditches run unnaturally straight through private woods I may not enter. Unnaturally straight blue lines on the green U.S. Geological Survey maps reveal these ditches to be Porcher's current headwaters, extending her watershed by hundreds of acres. Today untended and ignored, these were once the marvel of modern science, guaranteed to rid Carolina once and for all of the scourge of mosquitoes.

Mosquito ditches are contemporaneous with the halcyon days of DDT. Swamp after swamp was ditched and drained; what couldn't be drained was oiled to suffocate mosquito larvae. Everywhere hung a heavy fog of DDT. We children called the DDT truck "the fogging machine," and when it made its regular rounds, we would pursue it, running gleefully through the blue-white cloud it trailed. Our father had his own fogger attached to the lawnmower and, before picnics and parties, he ran round and round the yard, his mower spouting blue smoke.

Nothing worked. Drainage ditches clogged and puddled, becoming miles-long mosquito breeder ponds. The slightest breeze carried the fog off into the marsh, replacing chemicals with mosquitoes. DDT sank into the marsh, collecting in minute amounts in first this and then that animal, doubling its concentration in the shrimp or crab that devoured both these animals, then tripling in the fish that ate the shrimp and crab, quadrupling, and so on, working up the food chain, and reaching lethal levels in fish-eating pelicans and eagles, both of which nearly disappeared from our coasts. Today, flocks of pelicans are commonplace on our beaches, and observant birders are almost guaranteed to spot an eagle. We can thank Rachel Carson for their return. Vilified and pilloried for *Silent Spring*, she stood her ground and, more than anyone else, saved our birds, whose DDT-laced generations have long since been supplanted by cleaner descendants. In the late sixties, after twenty years of spraying, Long Island marshes stored some thirteen pounds of DDT per acre. How much yet lingers in Porcher's muds, leaching into the water and then into the oysters, and then into we who eat the oysters? How much remains stored in my fat cells? How much poison that I inhaled forty years ago passed with my sperm into my daughter and son?

As slowly as the DDT dissipates, the mosquito ditches dissolve, wasting away with every rain. Few humans visit them today, the only paths here those of coon and deer. Where once salt marsh lined a meandering tidal creek, a government-straightened ditch rushes through what has become freshwater loving black rush whose needle-sharp tips threaten blindness to the stumbling hiker. Spartina cordgrass battles to keep a toehold, and fiddlers burrow into the dikes, hastening their collapse. Raccoons foraging here last night ripped up a dozen burrows, further eroding the banks. I slip and slide through the mud, contributing in my own way to the demolition of an historical faux pas.

Neglected and slowly filling in, these ditches still drain fresh water that runs tea-brown over sand. Down where the salt marsh proper begins, they join in a local version of the Blue and White Niles with an unditched tributary whose greyish salt water is too silt-laden to see through. Entirely tidal, this branch rises and falls, changing its direction every six hours. Fed by swamps, the ditched heads of Porcher's always run seaward, their lower reaches fighting the rising tide for dominion.

Abandoned and all but forgotten, the old farming and mosquito ditches fill slowly as their dikes erode. Yet centuries more will pass before they are completely gone. In the meantime, legal battles swirl over who owns them and what one can do with them. "Ditches," their ostensible owners argue; "public wetlands," the state retorts. That the state constitution guarantees public access to all navigable salt waters raises the ante. Are these ditches fresh or salt? Brackish seems a reasonable compromise. Yet when you stand to lose or gain thousands of acres, you are unlikely to be reasonable. Lawyers want to know: salt or fresh? Public or private?

Should these waters be fresh, they can be channeled, diverted, dammed, diked, filled in, dug out, done whatever you damn well please with. Should they be salt, they're better protected. Walking the nearby golf course gives ample evidence of the difference. Porcher's Bluff resembles a sadistic puzzle piece, with enough indents and outdents to confuse a master puzzler. This is marsh, untouchable, unfillable, undrainable. The land itself, however, resembles a golf course anywhere: fake hills and ponds dot a manicured lawn. The developers have completely altered the watershed to provide recreation for hoards indifferent to Porcher's. They have dug ponds and lakes where there were none. Pretty blue ponds with banks steep enough and depths deep enough to hinder cattail and rush and algae. Ponds unnatural hereabouts, ponds relatively devoid of local flora and fauna. The spoil from these ponds has gone to fill in low areas—wetlands—to build hills and bunkers, sand traps and fairways. We might be in Minnesota, but we are, unfortunately, in Carolina.

Provided there's a current, freshwater swamps are cool, bugless havens where overarching trees temper the sun in a green shade made for shorts and t-shirts; but ponds excavated to provide water hazards for golf courses and waterfront lots for developers are still, stagnant, fresh, and full year round—perfect mosquito factories. People who build next to such ponds quickly discover the benefits of screened porches, which are the only way they can sit outdoors even in December.

The Indians had taught the first settlers what developers used to the closed windows of air conditioning cannot know—the blessings of a sea breeze. Every house worth a damn on the coast is built to catch the sea breeze which, in addition to cooling, keeps the mosquitoes at bay. Morning and evening breezes make life outdoors possible. Without them, life is hell; walking to the car means offering your body up as a blood sacrifice. Long pants and long sleeved shirts are de rigueur. Not that these stop mosquitoes; I learned long ago to wear a t-shirt under my shirt after suffering their stings and arrows.

Developers nonetheless insist upon altering the natural lay of the land, and gouging out mosquito factories they miscall lagoons. Our wetlands await the bulldozer. They will come; what politician will resist the siren call to sell our birthright for a mess of pottage? Already the blue sewer pipes are being laid, deals cut, tax dollars allocated. God-like and most un-Solomonic bureaucrats divide the dry land from the wet; before the ink dries on their Judas documents, mechanical caterpillars will eat up Porcher's.

13

Longleafs

My father remembers when Highway 17, the main road past Porcher's, was still paved in oyster shell, and allows as how it took "all goddamned day" to go thirty miles on it. Highway 17 today is a four-lane divided highway increasingly choked with cars travelling fifty-five miles an hour, subdivisions, and random businesses. Forty years ago it was still a two-lane country road. He used to drive us to town along it, past Grog Pond. Grog Pond was freshwater, and that was something the horses in my father's youth looked forward to. He remembers pulling off the road into the pond to water the horses. In the hollow of a swamp gum, the farmers kept a bottle of grog for themselves. The man who emptied it was honor bound to buy a replacement from the bootleggers when he got to town.

Highway 17 dates back to colonial days. The king commanded a highway built along the coast; it was called the King's Highway. Twentieth-century engineers, straightening with machines what the slaves had built by hand, abandoned long sections of the original roadbed. One of these led off through the woods near Grog Pond, and I used to travel it as a kid, sharing its gloomy lanes with Indians and pirates, Francis Marion and Redcoats, slaves and planters. I would pick up an oyster shell and wonder who hauled it there, slave or freeman, fifty or a hundred years ago.

You can see my father's kind of road yet if you go to the National Forest, where there are still rutted two-lane roads that keep to the sandy ridges for mile after mile of look-alike longleaf pine savannah. I learned to drive on these roads, Daddy taking me back in the woods where all I could hurt was pine trees. You could see daylight through the floorboards of our Chevy station wagon and, when the creeks were up after a rain, the water would come through. Daddy always said not to worry unless a crawfish crawled in with the water.

Water dark and cold as ice tea swirled round my shoes as I learned "for Christ's sake, don't stop in the middle of the god-damned creek." Creeks ran brown with tannin in my childhood woods. They say now you should never drink from streams, and no doubt they are right. A hundred feet up a drink-me stream I've come across a cow who died in childbirth, she and her calf's decaying innards spilled in water clear as distilled, but contaminated. Today cows are the least you have to worry about; in Carolina, folks who pump septic systems have been known to empty their trucks in creeks at night. When I was young, I didn't think of such things; a tea-dark stream was a drink-me stream. I drank from it, supposing the tannin cured the water of whatever corruption it carried.

Two-laned roads run straight as an old maid's back in church, on and on through woods so look-alike you're apt to get lost in them. Longleaf pines still reign in the Francis Marion National Forest, though their dominion is much reduced from colonial days. Loblolly is the foresters' current favorite, and its great plantations have replaced millions of acres of longleaf. "Pine deserts," we call these "tree farms"; nothing but pines grow in them, and those get clear cut every thirty years.

If you can find a uncut stand of old growth longleaf, you've come as close to paradise as you will this side of the grave. Tall, straight-trunked, and branchless for a hundred feet or more, longleafs rise like columns in a blue-roofed cathedral vaster than anything in Europe. Six to ten feet around at base, their fire-blackened bark blends into cinnamon higher up. Arch your back and look up ten stories to where branches reach out. Stretching off to the distance where they lose their form in a smokey blue haze of pine, longleaf trunks rising out of a calf-high carpet of grass and huckleberry. Listen: the wind soughs through the branches, playing the music of heaven-hummed needles.

"Bury me where the pines will sing me to sleep," my father asked. We have agreed to, and could have until two years ago when the forest service clear-cut the land around his childhood church. Built two hundred fifty years ago, it used to be a break in the forest monotony, a sudden glimpse of humanity on a road so deserted you thought yourself lost. The pines sang its dead

to sleep, promising sweet dreams until the end of time, fulfilling God's promise to Isaiah, "the glory of Lebanon shall come unto thee, the fir tree, the pine
tree, and the box together, to beautify the place of my sanctuary; and I will
make the place of my feet glorious." Money is as green as trees, though, and
buzzsaws screamed my father's ancestors awake as a forest fell. My son may
see the forest return, though neither my father nor I will live long enough to
hear it sing again. Willa Cather once wrote that only in graveyards did the
prairie remain; perhaps in Carolina, only in graveyards do longleafs still hum
in much-muted tones their ancient comforts.

14

Of Bays and Gators

Flying home, I know I'm near when the contoured fields disappear, the soil turns gray, and giant ovals pockmark the land. From the air, they resemble irrigated fields out west, green circles, though most are more oval than circular. Many are fields, drained and plowed under years ago. Only from the air can you trace their ghost impressions under furrows ignorant of the ancient landscape. Some still hold water, their cypress visible from thousands of feet up. On most of these, though, fields and tree farms encroach. A precious few, less than a dozen, are protected in parks.

These are Carolina bays; unique landforms, they occur nowhere else on earth but on our Atlantic coast. Americans travel thousands of miles, spend thousands of dollars, to see less rare landforms. No explanation of their origins satisfies everyone. Today's scientific fashion favors their formation by prevailing winds scouring natural depressions—or offshore currents eddying in shallow seas—or sinkholes. The public's favorite theory, though discarded by the savants, is a monster meteorite shower bombarding the Coastal Plain with a hundred thousand bombs. First suggested in the 1930s, the meteorite theory remained popular into the fifties, cited by Velikovsky as proof of his cosmic cataclysm. That no one has ever found a meteorite fragment has been explained by substituting a killer comet for a monster meteorite.

Whatever their origin, the bays owe their demise to man. Time was filling them in anyway, but it is sad to see a distinctive geological feature disappear for the sake of money.

Those that have been dated range in age from four thousand to forty thousand years, with estimates of undated bays' ages ranging from two hundred fifty thousand years to perhaps one and a half million years old. Young or old, the cypress and moss choked bays seem ancient, older than time itself. Like all truly old things, they are profoundly sad. Grey cypress grips the buried bottom with claw-like buttresses. A tangle of knees rise into the air, staring like scarf-covered widows and orphans of a war, standing like forlorn passengers at a bus stop. Downed trunks cross each other, unable to rot. Cypress lasts forever, and the bay preserves an antediluvian past before man and mammal.

Science fiction abounds with dreams of time travel. Travel to a Carolina bay and sit a while, and you will boldly go where no one has gone before. Fast-paced, hot-blooded mammal that you are, slow down, relax, laze in the sun until the man and mammal within sink to sleep, and the reptile that lies hid beneath your human forebrain and mammalian midbrain awakens, rouses itself, slinks up from the stygian depths of your own hind-brain to greet a day and an environment like those it knew when you were not even yet a nightmare to frighten dragons dozing in the sun.

Those dragons still live in Carolina. We call them alligators. Colonial accounts record monsters as long as twenty-three feet; like much else, today's are shrunk in size, the largest I have seen was perhaps fifteen feet long. American traveler and botanist William Bartram recorded in 1791 his impression of an alligator: "Behold him rushing forth from the flags and reeds. His enormous body swells. His plaited tail brandished high, floats upon the lake. The waters like a cataract descend from his opening jaws. Clouds of smoke issue from his dilated nostrils. The earth trembles with his thunder." Today the best place to hear such roars is in Florida's alligator farms. There, penned and corralled, bulls still roar, "not only shaking the air and waters, but causing the earth to tremble; and when hundreds and thousands are roaring at the same time, you can scarcely be persuaded but that the whole globe is violently and dangerously agitated."

Alligators still roar in Carolina swamps. A few miles north of Porcher's, Bull Island is home to what some claim is the thickest concentration of alligators in the state. They possess every patch of the island's water. Twelve foot behemoths sun on mudbanks, five footers float in weed-choked canals, and foot-long yearlings scramble through the cattails.

Alligators live in Porcher's fresh headwaters and fish its salt waters. Gator crawls snake through the mucky swamps, sneak across the upper marsh. Their trails wear broad valleys in the old levees. An alligator [el lagarto, or lizard, in Spanish] looks something like a gigantic lizard, and his track resembles a lizard's, paws on either side of a tail drag. When a clawed pawprint engulfs your out-spread hand, though, you realize the limits of cousinship. You look around: where is the beast who made these tracks?

My sister has an alligator skull on her television. It's a small skull, a little over a foot long. You can figure its owner was five or six times longer. I fin-ger its teeth, especially the longer tusks that grace the upper jaw, and stick my arm between its jaws and wonder, could they, living, have severed my arm?

Porcher's is the alligators' main highway from swamp to marsh, from home to market. They float down with the ebbing tide; six hours later, they return, floating upstream with the rising tide. Some ride high, head, body and tail half showing. Others ride lower, nostrils and eyes awash. I like to think these latter ones are heavy with food, fish and crab they have found in the same holes I fish.

When I was young, I'd come upon their tracks on the sandbars of a hole. Young and alone, I'd look out at the dark water I had to wade into; what lurked in its depths beside fish and shrimp and crabs? Bartram witnessed an alligator fishing expedition: "I have seen an alligator take up out of the water several great fish at a time, and just squeeze them betwixt his jaws, while the tails of the great trout flapped about his eyes and lips, ere he had swallowed them. The horrid noise of their closing jaws, their plunging amidst the bro-ken banks of fish, and rising with their prey some feet upright above the water, the floods of water and blood rushing out of their mouths, and the clouds of vapor issuing from their wide nostrils, were truly frightful."

Porcher's erupts, an alligator swinging round and round, sweeping water and fish and shrimp in a confused jumble, while he, like an armor-plated dog, chases his great tail round and round, grabbing at mullet. Ten minutes later, the water is calm, the only trace of ambush and massacre confused scrapings on the sand and a gator crawl upcreek.

Alligators bound for home congregate upstream of my sister's dock, wait-ing for tide to crest. At full tide, they beach and slow crawl their way through blackberry and bramble to dry land and the ponds they call home.

Those homes used to be deep in the swamp, but Porcher's developer excavated ponds deeper and bigger than anything an alligator could dig.

Porcher's swamps are empty today, their alligators now living on the golf course. Sarah and I spotted one sunning on the bank of the golf course's largest pond. Nearby was a dead oak, its branches filled with cormorants hung out to dry. A dozen turtles sunned on the trunk, lunch in the gator's eyes, unless the great white heron, frozen in fishing pose, were more to his taste.

Such stuff must go. Developers plan houses for this pond. Hence the trees must be leveled, for what's the point of a waterfront lot if you can't see the water? With the trees will go the cormorants. The turtles will still sun where they can, though there will never again be dozens in a tree. The gator, too, will go, but at his own pace, in his own good time, seeking a more secluded hole to call home. He and his kind are survivors; they are older than the golf courses, older than Porcher's Bluff, older than the shell rings, older than the bays, older than Porcher's Creek itself. They will endure.

15

Shark Hole

To my siblings and myself, the creek was our Eden. Like Raleighs on our personal Orinoco, were we to wade it far enough, back through time and tide, we might, just might, recover our childhood, the time before my father disappeared. Each creek becomes THE creek, each wade a sacrament, a sacred ritual whose right repetition might break the spell, restoring father, childhood, innocence, and family.

Wading the creek, you discover it winds and turns on itself, snaking, seeking through the marsh. A hundred feet by crow becomes five hundred by fish, and what on terra firma would be a two minute stroll becomes a half hour slog through mud and shell up to your knees or worse. Porcher's wiggles like a worm fresh stuck on a hook.

Walking its marshy upper reaches is an exercise in frustration. Horseshoe bends abound; you must make a pact with yourself to follow the creek bed, not to short cut cross the bends' necks. I have walked a hundred mazy, muddy feet in order to make a ten foot headway. Back when I was young and time precious, I would cut every horseshoe bend I could. The creek has followed me, where I followed raccoons, who took a nightly shortcut so often they wore a path. Where our passage killed the marsh back so that its peaty roots were exposed, the tide has tugged this way and that, wearing the roots out till mere mud lay open to the water's seduction. In twenty years, the creek decapitated several horseshoe bends, cutting a new channel. The old channel fills with mud two feet deep, the consistency of a puree.

Erosion is kid's play this far up Porcher's. A thousand turns and returns downriver, the grownup creek bulldozes its way through proper bluffs, undercutting live oaks and cedars in its chase for its tail. The creek bed reflects the current's path. One side of the creek is steep: the current cuts close to shore here. The other side shelves gently, beach-like where the current is slack. Here there are mud snails and fiddlers, there there are fiddlers and abrupt bluffs. Halfway between each bend the current crosses from one side of the creek to the other. Where it crosses over are shallows.

Should you use the creek for transport, you need to know this. Try swimming upstream on an ebb tide and you soon enough learn to appreciate slack water and back eddies when you find them. The creek's inhabitants know this already. If you plan to fish these waters, you must learn what they know. Look for shrimp in slack water, where they'll be feeding on muddy bottom.

In fall, nighttime Charleston Harbor resembles more a Japanese than an American port. Two hundred bobbing lights decorate its shallows. Fishermen anchor in the mud flats under the giant roller coaster ramparts of the Charleston bridges. With a half-opened can of dog food as bait, they wait for shrimp and cast again and again as long as the tide allows. On a good night they can catch several bushels of shrimp. The next day, many will sell them, illegally, from the back of their parked pickups; they're almost always fresher than those caught by the trawlers.

Of course you need a boat to shrimp like this—or even to shrimp the mud flats of Porcher's. I didn't often have a boat, so I learned to fish the holes. The creek is filled with holes. Low tide, you learn them, where they are, how deep they are, what kind of bottom, what obstructions, whatever you can.

Some holes are legendary. Shark Hole, for example; at eighty feet, it's the deepest place in Charleston County. Even the harbor hasn't depths this profound. Not that you can see them—the water's so murky with mud and life visibility is measured in inches. Dive under and try it yourself; the surface disappears a foot down, and you can't see your hand an arm's length in front of your face.

They don't call it Shark Hole for nothing, either. Fools fish it for shark—and catch them. There are over twenty-five different species in South Carolina, according to fishing regulations. To fish for shark, you need steel leaders thick enough so your catch can't bite through it—and ten- or twelve-inch hooks large enough to hold them—and blood to call them in. Although some experts counsel women not to swim when they're having their period, so sensitive to the least amount of blood are sharks, shark fishers don't swallow this idea of subtle attraction. They heave enough bloody chum overboard to color the water around their boat. They want everything that likes blood to know they're there.

Daddy claimed Shark Hole hides more than sharks. The sharks will dispose of whatever you throw them. They're a convenient place to hide a corpse you don't want washing ashore. People have found old license plates, crab pot buoys, parts of horse, and shoes, human shoes, some with feet still in them, in the stomachs of sharks.

The film "Jaws" ruined places like Shark Hole for me. Anytime I'm in water too deep or too dark to see bottom, I wonder what's down there, especially as my means of getting around is generally an inner tube. Surfers paddling off California are said to look like seals to prowling sharks. I wonder what my toes resemble dangling off one end of an inner tube, and my ample butt bull's-eyed by rubber?

Sand shark carcasses are plentiful on the beach, where fishermen toss them to die. Down at the docks, you can generally cadge a small shark from the trawlers who bring them up in their nets—or buy one from the seafood store. They're worth buying, if only to admire the sandpaper skin, the sleek, predator lines, the blue upper body, more beautifully camouflaged than the killer attack subs that used to sneak out of Charleston Harbor. Run your finger along multiple rows of teeth so fine they are beautiful, nearly cute—until you remember "Jaws" and remind yourself there are near relatives that could bite you in half if they cared to.

Seven miles from Shark Hole you can find traces of such less cuddly sharks. Where I grew up is really a narrow peninsula, a spit of sand between the Wando River and the marshes, creeks, and sounds that lie behind the barrier islands. Along the Wando and several other rivers near Charleston are "fossil beaches," lowtide beaches where the current washes up fossils from one hundred thousand to twenty million years ago. Clams, oysters, snails, turtles, and rays mingle remains with horse and tree and elephant—and shark. Hundreds of shark teeth, many minute. Some a good two inches long, some four inches, and some giants six inches long. People who know such things estimate the latter came from sharks forty feet long, creatures bigger than the Great White Shark of today. I'm walking along, bent over as are all beachcombers. I pause, bend down, pick up a grey-black tooth dropped from a shark with mouth so large I could stand in it. Thank God he died twenty million years ago.

Then I look out across the water, the dark, impenetrable water. Water that leads to places where the coelacanth lurks. I can't help but wonder how they know, really know, that the Greater White eats no more.

I don't fish Shark Hole. Still, it's only two miles as the vulture flies, four as the shark swims, from there to here. I know that porpoise hunt this far up the creek; who is to say that I am safe, even here where the water shoals to two feet? People have died in less water than this—but you don't catch shrimp thinking like this. Avoid Shark Hole and its even deeper cousins, those that lie within yourself. Stay shallow, safe. There are surprises enough and secret depths even in lesser holes.

16

Big Hole

Good-sized tributaries into Lowcountry creeks invariably produce holes. You can watch from the bank or jump in and feel the eddies carry you round and round in a circle. That eddy cuts into the bottom, excavating and clearing out mud and sand and so making a nice hole. High tide will cover the creek with water from marshy bank to marshy bank. Low water, you can be standing on creek bottom, water barely wetting you feet. Two feet in front of you the bottom will disappear, dropping down up to twelve feet. Deep enough and dark enough to make you think twice about swimming in it.

We called my father's favorite hole the Big Hole. It formed where the creek makes a t-junction, its main trunk branching right and left, each arm snaking its way towards its swampy headwaters, one arm brown with tannin, the other grey with mud.

Creek life congregates in holes at low tide. The prevailing theory among creekers is that the shrimp and all are trapped in the holes, deluded by their greater depth into supposing there's plenty of water everywhere, only to be stranded when the tide drops beneath a certain level.

No one, shrimp or human, likes scraping bottom. As a kid, I can remember the occasional Navy ship run aground on one of the more diabolical turns in the Charleston ship channel. A Navy captain once told me that only Philadelphia, some hundred miles from the ocean, has a worse channel than Charleston. One can always let the harbor pilot skipper his ship through the channel, and plenty of civilian skippers do; but the military, being military, had to do it themselves. Upstream of Charleston Harbor's Hog Island, the channel cuts hard to port, then immediately, and as hard, to starboard. When the tide's going out, the Wando will push you against the Hog Island shoals, and the Cooper, which you're trying to ascend, will send you towards Hog Island as well. Add to this a wind from the wrong quarter, and a harbor neophyte has his hands full. He can't pick and choose his time of approach; the bridge is so low that some ships can't even get under it at high tide. The channel's barely deep enough at half tide for others; windows of opportunity come narrow and shallow in Charleston Harbor.

Each hole has its own character, and you get to know them personally and individually walking the creek. Dad's hole is near perfect: no shell to snag a net on, some relic roots off to one side, but that's muddy bottom anyway. Nothing in the center but water, deep water. Charleston Harbor heats up to seventy to eighty degrees in the summer. Marshes get even hotter, resembling as they do baking sheets filled with water and left out in the sun. Nothing to do but soak up heat. A shallow, sandy hole will heat to bath water temperature on a windless day, but a deep hole will always have a thermal gradient. Like a pond, the deeper water will be noticeably cooler than the top layer. You can feel the difference if you walk out into a hole. Swim out and you dangle your toes down in the dark, cool water, imagining what it must feel like to swim in the middle of the ocean, nothing between you and the abyss but ever-colder water and whatever swims by.

In a good hole, like Dad's, you can feel the shrimp. Wade out and stand still. They will school around you and start nibbling your bare flesh. Little pin pricks. You're being eaten alive. I wonder if a Chinese emperor even tried torture by shrimp? Newcomers to the creek dislike the feeling; Sarah will not tolerate a hundred shrimp bumping into her legs and gnawing on them. Shrimping's a different matter. You want to feel them; it's a sign of a rich hole. A good cast will spread out in a circle and sink straight to the bottom. The shrimp can feel the mesh sinking on them, and they dart, out and up; but there's nowhere to go. You can tell a good haul before you see it by waiting to feel the net's slight tremor as a school of shrimp bump into the collar trying to escape. You keep fishing it until you can't feel them, until every single shrimp that dared gnaw you is in your bucket.

17

Gulf Stream

On midsummer's full moon tides, what few turtles remain return to lay their eggs on Carolina's barrier beaches. Our houses have destroyed their beaches, our dogs and cats eaten their eggs, our moon-like streetlights lured their young landward to death, our shrimpers drowned some who swam into their nets, our castoff plastic bags choked those who thought them jellyfish. I myself killed dozens of potential turtles, eating scrambled turtle eggs and turtle egg pancakes when young.

Daddy took me out as a child to see the turtles come ashore. As evening came on, we motored out to the uninhabited barrier beaches, grilled fresh-caught mullet on a driftwood fire colored green and red and blue from secret sea salts and minerals, watched the moon rise out of the darkening ocean and draw behind it to the beach six sea turtles big enough for me to ride.

We've all seen films of these beasts lumbering up out of the surf; but to be a child, with the moon lighting up the palmetto-fringed beach, and a warm sea breeze in your face, to watch the wet beasts glisten as they crawl up the shelving beach through the low surf, to touch the strangeness that is an ocean-going turtle's barnacled carapace, to have her reptile eyes regard you with indifference, to watch her silent excavation and her body, immobilized, laying a hundred potential lives, and then to look into the dunes and see the gathering raccoons and know that none of these eggs will live beyond tonight is to realize how unimportant—and how fortunate—one's own life is.

Nowadays, if you like the turtles, you should not go out to the beaches to witness their return, so tenuous is their hold on our coast. Turtle teams relocate or shelter nests with chicken wire enclosures to keep out coons and dogs and cats, and cooperative beachfront dwellers keep their houses dark during hatching season; but there are too few cages and cooperative islanders, and too many dogs, cats, coons and uncooperative islanders. The only turtle I've seen recently is a grizzled mother who'd swum into Copahee and taken my hook. She took half an hour to land and, when I got her close enough to cut the line, I saw that I was the third fisherman to leave his hook in her face. The only crawls I've seen have been days-old tracks above high water mark that led into the dune's edge. The only eggs I've seen have been empty, their ragged shells littering the sand where four-footed varmints had feasted.

These vanishing visitors are not the only creatures who return. The shad return each year with spring, their arrival anticipated by the shad tree's white blooms. Driving to work in Virginia, I spy in the woods their white announcement that the year is young again, the earth reborn, and know that the Santee, Edisto, Combahee, Peedee, and Ashepoo are thick with fish. It is time to cook my father shad roe. My sister cannot abide seafood, but she suffers shad roe's salty taste and fishy odor for the sake of our father, whose yearly consumption of a hundred thousand unborn shad may be one of the secrets of his longevity. The roe lies like two purplish grey sausages encased in clear membranes fretted with red blood vessels on either side of the female shad's intestinal cavity. Shad itself is a fishbone nightmare—the only way to eat it is to cook it long enough to dissolve the bones—but we sauté the roe in mere minutes and serve it hot with hominy grits. Daddy, his tongue still savoring what it has tasted each spring for the last eighty years, looks up and asks, as he always does, "I wonder what the poor folk are eating tonight?"

Shad do not run Porcher's—she is too small a creek for them—but eels do. They inhabit even landlocked ponds in the Lowcountry. I remember as a child catching them on autumn nights by hand as they snaked through the grass from a pond overland to a ditch twenty feet away, whose barely damp bottom led through fields and woods eventually to the creek. Most fishermen in America resent hooking eels, but smoked eel is delicious, as the Dutch know, who import huge quantities of Chesapeake Bay eel. I remember walking Amsterdam's streets, peeling back the skin and nibbling my way down smoked eels' backbones the way I might gnaw a corn dog in America.

Shad, eels and turtles. The sea is filled with seasoned travelers. Even the mullet I net winter elsewhere. My childhood eels swam up Porcher's from spawning grounds in the legendary Sargasso Sea, leagues beyond the Bermudas. I too return to my natal waters, pulled by a lure composed of mud and sand and salt.

Sarah tolerates my homing habits, although she thinks there are better beaches than mine, clearer creeks, and less buggy marshes. She shows me fifty miles of uninhabited white sand beach at Hatteras, and raises her eyes to heaven when I prefer my house-choked, muddy-watered, mosquito-infested beaches. Like the eel and shad and turtle and mullet, sea bass and trout, shrimp and crabs, my home waters draw me. Scientists surmise magnetism and celestial navigation draw us. More mystic musers suppose the "taste" of our waters lures us home. I side with these.

My birth waters mingle with the Atlantic's, flow hither and yon, ever more attenuated, ever fainter, like childhood's memories, fading, almost forgotten—when a chance odor, taste, sight, sound, or feel conjures a world and draws me decades back. When a nearly-spent Hurricane Hugo passed over Virginia, I quit my house to stand in torrential rains as warm as bath water, warmth that bathed me in a memory of childhood showers. Had I not had neighbors or inhibitions, I might have shed clothes and decades and danced naked like I did as a child, bathed in memories. Of such mystic warmth wrote Charleston poet Henry Timrod on the eve of the Civil War in his poem "Ethnogenesis," describing the Gulf Stream as "that vast gulf which lips our Southern strand,/ And through the cold, untempered ocean pours/ Its genial streams, that far off Arctic shores/ May sometimes catch upon the softened breeze/ Strange tropic warmth and hints of summer seas."

Still a marvel to us, imagine what the Gulf Stream must have seemed to those who witnessed its discovery. I take out my stepson Nicholas' battered globe, and trace with my finger the Gulf Stream's course from Florida north along my coast, up to Hatteras and Cape Cod, where geography, the Newfoundland Current, and the spinning earth force the world's mightiest river eastward, into the North Atlantic, where passengers aboard the QE2 shed their northern sweaters to bask in the Stream's warmth. She washes Ireland and Britain, and palm trees grow a thousand miles farther north in Europe than in America. The Scilly Isles bloom year-round, their Stream-bathed climate a taste of far-off tropics for the fog-bound English. Turning south, she skirts France, returning home to me when I buy wines made of grapes nourished by rains blown in from off her heaving bosom, wines like Keats imagined,

"Tasting of Flora and the country green,/ Dance, and Provencal song, and sunburnt mirth!" Farther south, she sweetens Portuguese port, and steeps the magic islands of the Azores, Canaries, and Madeiras.

The Gulf Stream warms four continents, some twenty nations; who knows how many millions of people's lives are mellowed by her waters. She mingles waters from the Rio Grande, the Missouri and Mississippi, the Tombigbee and the Alabama, the Everglades, the Savannah, the Cape Fear and the Roanoke, the James, the Potomac and the Susquehannah, the Hudson and the Housatonic, the St. Lawrence and the St. John's, the Shannon and the Liffey, the Wye and the Avon, the Seine, the Loire, the Gironde, the Guadalquivir, the Senegal and the Niger, the Amazon and the Orinoco. To this torrent Porcher's contributes.

John Donne would have no man an island, all of us part of the main, the land. No doubt we are, but we are all also part of the sea that washes our shores. Though but a tiny invagination, Porcher's is nonetheless a part of that great stream, and washes shores distant in space and time.

Astronomers tell us the light we see from the stars is ancient, sometimes billions of years in passage from there to here. Who has measured the passage of Porcher's waters? How long did the salty mouthful I swallow take in its coming hither? Where will it go when I piss it back? Did dinosaurs once bathe in this water when it lapped the shores of vanished continents? Did it wash Noah's Ark, rain upon Jesus when he slept upon the sea? Did Moby Dick spit on Ahab with what I now swallow? Did Huckleberry Finn swim in it when it was fresh?

A student I once knew traced the secret origins of springs by placing dyes in far off sinkholes and waiting to see which ones appeared within a given spring. There are no dyes to trace the origins or destinations of Porcher's waters. Imagination alone can make that trek.

Geologists suppose Porcher's to be at least six thousand years old; that is when the rising sea slowed and allowed the formation of long, narrow barrier islands from seaborne sands behind which lay shallow lagoons such as Copahee and Gray's. Creeks such as Porcher's formed at the heads of these lagoons, reaching farther inland, some dead-ending and wholly salt, others draining fresh water swamps. Many experts suppose global warming will accelerate the sea's rise; if so, creeks like Porcher's will grow longer as they follow the topography up and into the woods, eventually meeting the Wando, whose creeks reach within a mile of Porcher's. Then the barrier islands, gifts of the sea, will have been reclaimed, and my stomping grounds, once part of the mainland but now surrounded by water, will have become itself an island.

Bull, Caper's, Dewee's, the Isle of Palms, and Sullivan's may all disappear long before a rising sea islands Porcher's Bluff. These islands resist the sea's pull thanks to the sediments the Santee River just to the north pours into the Atlantic. In 1942, the U. S. Army Corps of Engineers, to general acclaim, dammed the Santee; since then, the river has lost nine hundred feet of shoreline, and Bull, Caper's and Dewee's Islands have begun to disappear. Seventy five percent of Carolina's shoreline is eroding, in part thanks to such misguided efforts to "control" nature.

Porcher's flows, indifferent to such erosion. I like to think that she remembers flowing miles farther eastward before the rising sea ate up her lower reaches, she herself once a mighty river. Where shark and whale swim today, mammoth and mastodon, saber tooth and cave bear roamed. Tribes unguessed, unnamed, unknown, hunted boreal forests now sunk beneath sea and sand. Perhaps, equipped with aqualung and submarine, I could trace the fossil course of Usquatach or Quezasolitle Seepahowatchie or some such uncouth combination of sounds, Porcher's great-great-great-great-grandriver running under the smooth sands of Dewee's Island.

Dewee's and her sister barrier islands drift south along the coast, carried by a littoral current hundreds of miles long. The islands erode on their northern ends, accrete on their southern; Bull Island, having lost its north end lighthouse, reaches a sandy finger south towards Caper's, whose beachfront recedes each year, chasing Dewee's, whose beaches pursue the Isle of Palms, whose high rise hotels will someday disappear beneath the eroding sea, as their island grasps at the ever-escaping Sullivan's.

Huge though it be, this coastal current is but an eddy of the Gulf Stream, an incidental moment of turbulence in the great river's rush north. Science tells us the continents themselves spin round the globe, like leaves caught on a current, jostling one another's shoulders, some sinking, some riding high over others, some drifting off on lonely trajectories of them own. The earth too spins hither and yon, as does the solar system, and the galaxy, and the local group of galaxies, and the universe itself, for all I know. Round and round and round, returning to the beginning only to begin again.

Who knows where or when that beginning is? For me, Porcher's is always the beginning. Yet mullet return to Beaufort south of me, turtles to Winyah Bay north of me; Sarah returns to Hatteras, and tourists to Myrtle Beach. Every where is some thing's home water. When Porcher's dies, as die she must, other creeks will take her place, sheltering mullet and shad and eel and, should we humans become responsible, turtles and, with luck, small boys to wonder at them.

18

Frogs

Spring where I grew up meant a palimpsest of the squished corpses of piggy-backing frogs littering the highway. I remember looking with curiosity and pity upon the near-perfect match of body upon body, heads just out of alignment like a double exposure. When these corpses dried out, I'd peel them off the highway like decals and bring them home to marvel at—until Mother would discover my collection and throw them out, forbidding me to collect any more leapfrogs.

A few days after squashed frog season, the world was awash in blobs, globs, ropes and necklaces of frog spawn, thousands of green-black gems set in egg-white floating in every wet spot in the woods. Years later I learned the connection between piggybacking frogs and frog eggs, but in my happy youth, they were miracles, as were the soon-to-arrive tadpoles, every pond fringed with a living necklace of black, every drying puddle choked with asphyxiating frogs in the making. Our pond's margin was a tadpole interstate, a hundred thousand heads, each shaking a tail, in constant motion. We would dip a kitchen tumbler into their midst and fish out ten to twenty at a time. Visiting the pond daily, we watched these pollywogs transmogrify, sprouting tiny hind feet and fore feet, diminishing tails, and elongating head and body until miniature frogs the size of my fingernail swam before us.

These were all frogs to us as children, though now I know them to have been Eastern spade foot toads, creatures who burrow six inches to a foot into the sandy Lowcountry soil, and remain hidden and quiescent until a heavy rain. Then legions of them appear, mate, spawn in a rush, and are gone. Behind our house a dip in the ground filled with water—and toads—after heavy rains. We wore ear plugs and ran fans to mask the night-long squawking keer-r-raw of a thousand males desperate to mate before dawn.

Our father took us out on such nights, armed with flashlights whose beams revealed a world awash in amphibia. From every wet nook in the grass, yellow-green eyes regarded us. The very ground seemed to heave its back as a thousand toads hopped and crawled and croaked and leapt from back to back in imitation of our playground games. Delighted, we children dropped our flashlights and become ourselves leaping frogs, ribbiting and knee-deeping as we leapt over each other. Our shadows slowly changing shape, legs elongating, necks shrinking, backs hunching, we might have been the gods of amphibia summoned by a thousand singing devotees.

Later, when we were bathing, Daddy told us stories of children he had known who had leapfrogged too long into such summer nights and could not, when they would, return to their human shapes. "Look at your hands," he said. "They're already wrinkling up like a frog's." So they were, the skin hanging from them, soft and pliable, half-frog already. "Had you played out in the night much longer, who knows? Perhaps you would have grown webs. Come on, you've stayed too long in the water as it is." One by one, we hopped out to be dried off. "Frog gods can smell out children who have played leapfrog too long at night," Daddy continued, pulling the plug to drain the tub. "They live deep underground, and come up through drain pipes. Sometimes you can see them looking at you after you've let the water out the tub." Laughing at the joke the first time we heard it, one of us looked down the tub drain and screamed. We all looked and there, blinking back at us, was a yellow-rimmed eye.

The eye still watches. From time to time, and tub to tub, I can see it, if I remember to look, and if luck is with me. My skeptic half explains such eyes away as water dropping down the drainpipe; but the child within knows better and, after a long relaxing soak when I discover my skin wrinkling, and what might be webbing at the base of my fingers, I know what I will see watching me after I let the water out—a dark, fathomless eye rimmed in the yellow-green colors of amphibia. Just to be safe, I then confine myself to showers, and do not walk abroad late at night when the frogs are singing.

19

Plat-eye

A few miles north of Porcher's lies Seewee Bay, a muddy, marsh-bound version of Copahee visited today solely by oystermen. It takes its name from the Seewee Indians who occupied these shores when the English came in 1670. The English first gave the name Seewee to Bull's Bay, but soon enough switched names when the prestigious, and white, Bull family bought up the land, relegating Seewee to a muddy backwater.

John Lawson recorded five Seewee villages in his colonial passage through Carolina. He even visited the one at Walnut Grove, my father's family place. All five villages were deserted.

As Lawson tells the tale, the Seewees originally welcomed the white man, but soon enough they grew tired of being cheated in their dealings with him. They saw that his white-winged boats all came from the east, and so they decided to take their grievances to his king. For months they stored provisions in secret. The appointed day came, and the entire nation, saving those too old or too young, set sail in giant canoes for England—and vanished.

For how long did aging grandparents keep their growing fears from hapless grandchildren playing in the dirt of villages they'd soon forsake? The clay pot filled with periwinkles that my father's sister found in the mound at Walnut Grove: was this left behind by the last adult Seewee to leave the village as a gesture of despair, there being no need for periwinkles where he or she was doomed to go? Was it left in hope by a child who believed her parents would return and, returning, be hungry for their favorite meal of periwinkles?

We Leland children also waited their return. Camped upon shell islands we'd been told were Seewee village sites, we'd sit around a fire and rehearse the Seewee's sad history. As the fire died and the night grew, we scared each other with the tales our father had told us, of how you could listen late at night when the wind was off the sea and hear, faint and far away, the cries of drowning Indians, of how fishermen had reported seeing, when the moon was low and the tide high, dugouts filled with silent Indians, a skeleton crew whose feathered skulls grinned at their fleshy audience and vanished.

We never saw for sure those canoes but, hushing each other, we looked and listened. We heard things, far-off cries in the night, paddles stealthily dipped into water, the scrape of wooden hulls against marsh grass, and the whispered tread of moccasined feet approaching our campfire. We'd throw more wood on the fire, talk loud, hug ourselves in our sleeping bags, and be too scared to rise and pee in the night.

Daddy warned us not to listen too long to the Seewee. Their sibilant songs were seductive; like sirens, they could lure us seaward to wander with them through Atlantean forests lost a mile beneath the ocean's surface. Enough ships sink, planes vanish, swimmers disappear each year to substantiate such legends. The Bermuda Triangle, after all, lies just off shore.

Even grown, I hear them calling me. On the beach, I am drawn to snorkel beyond the breakers, out to where the surface rolls in gentle swells, and the water's clear and the bottom barely visible, where the sea turns from shallow green to profound blue, and I can feel the lure of the abyss. At such times it seems an easy thing to keep on swimming east, and I must force myself to stop and see just how far I've come. The shore has always receded farther than I thought, my human companions smaller, less real, the houses so distant through the shimmering air they seem under water, and drowning more attractive than swimming back. Should I dive now, sounding the bottom, the pressure builds, the world grows underwater quiet, and I hear voices singing, beckoning. Are these the Seewee or merely my pulse tom-tomming in my ears?

Others besides Indians haunt the night marsh. On calm and cloudless nights, the stars skinny dip, Cassiopeia, Andromeda, Perseus, and Cephus swimming with me in Porcher's. Stardust lingers long after the stars have fled, translating swimming humans into gods, bodies phosphorescing, dripping celestial gold. Jumping mullet trace golden ellipses in the night, schooling shrimp shine like silver slivers of fingernails, a thousand jellyfish shimmer like veiled dancers, and glowing arcs three or four feet long ascend the creek as some unknown sea creature humps its way towards me—and I drip gold as I jump back onto the dock.

I am never the only creature haunting the night creek. *Things* unheard of in science books hunt the marsh, and few people venture far from their docks after dark. "How many shrimp do you suppose you've eaten in your life," my father would ask me. "A thousand? A hundred thousand? Two hundred thousand? The god of shrimp knows, you can be sure. He keeps count and, one night, he will exact vengeance." Then he spun a tale I only half believed of gods created in the image of shrimp, god shrimp twice as long as a bateau, immortal crustaceans with bulging eyes and armored carapace and saw-toothed horns that came up creeks on the spring tides, when the channel was deep enough to hold their bulk, shrimp whose antennae stretched fifty feet in front of them, man-eating shrimp that fed on shrimpers careless enough to cast at night. Crabs large enough to rip a crabber's boat in half, known to have stuffed crabpots with human heads. Ferocious fiddlers with two-foot claws that tore careless fishermen limb from limb, baiting trees with their carcasses. Shark too—always shark. Twelve-footers frequented Porcher's lower reaches during daylight; who was to say what monsters swam up from Shark Hole at night? "Say you cut your finger on an oyster," my father would suppose over his evening Scotch. "You rinse it in the creek, go on shrimping, think nothing of it. But you rinse your finger every time you reach in the water to pull in your net, and the tide ebbs, carrying your blood seaward. How much blood do you think it take to call in whatever lives in Shark Hole?"

I was learning about the Egyptians at the time, about jackal-headed Anubis and crocodile-mouthed Seth. Shrimp-headed gods and giant crabs were equally credible. "Don't tell your Mother; she doesn't hold with gods besides Jesus. But when I was your age. . ." Dropping his voice, bending closer, his whiskey-rich breath in my face, Daddy described rituals of prevention, sacrifices one made to avert disaster, offerings to offended deities. Land dwellers eat sea creatures, and the sea gods eat terrestrial objects—liquor and red meat and certain vegetables offered at night, on an ebbing tide, on candle-lit platters floated downcreek to Shark Hole and other fathomless portals into worlds where humans are food for hungry gods.

God of gods and horror of horrors was the plat-eye. Gods that resembled creek creatures were one thing, mere exaggerations of the quotidian, but no one knew what the plat-eye looked like. To see it was to die. I had actually heard it. Daddy and I had been out shrimping in late September. Low tide and dusk had coincided, and we were late coming home, Daddy poling our bateau up Porcher's while I headed our catch. The herons had already flown off to their swamp roosts, and flocks of crows had passed overhead on their way to their island hideaways. Too tired to talk, we listened to the plops and gurgles of the creek as the shadows crept out of the marsh and the stars came out. Lulled to complacency, we were rounding a bend when a weird, unearthly screech accompanied by the sound of huge wings beating the night air scared hell out of me. Daddy stopped poling, sat slowly down in the stern, and let us drift. "That, son," he said in a whisper, "that was the plat-eye."

He told me of fishermen who'd gone into the marsh at night, never to return, of empty boats found the next morning adrift in the marsh, of bloated bodies washing up without eyes, the plat-eye's favorite food, of how it *preceded* humans up nighttime creeks, calling its kind in for the kill. As we floated up Porcher's, we heard, again and again, preceding us, its drawn-out hunting cry—cre-e-ahh-haugh, cre-e-ahh-haugh, cre-e-ahh-haugh—and the whoosh of ghost wings against the unyielding air.

Sketch a quick cross in the air and you avert the Devil; surround yourself with an unbroken circle of holy water and all the forces of hell cannot touch you; wear a cross round your neck and you can skirt graveyards with impunity; plant conchshells in your garden to ward off spirits; but nothing averts the plat-eye. It dines on souls it sucks out through its victims' nostrils, and desserts on eyes blinded by fear.

"Some say the plat-eye came from Africa with the slaves. That it learned to like human flesh during the long voyage west, feasting on corpses thrown overboard from slave ships. Others say it's older than slavery. That it ate red men long before it had white and black flesh to choose from. That it pre-dates the Indians even. That it came from somewhere else, hurled here or awakened, ripped from hell itself by the thousand meteorites that dug the bays." Daddy would take a long drink of Scotch, look out across the marsh to the Indian islands.

Then he'd cuss the archeologists who'd come out one summer, banned everyone from exploring "our" Indian islands, and dug them up themselves.

They carted off in the name of science boatloads of artifacts, hid them away on dusty university shelves, wrote scholarly suppositions on what they thought might be the function of what they found. Some supposed the islands shell middens—a fancy phrase for garbage dumps. Some reckoned them villages, and others thought them the site of unknown ceremonies.

My father already knew their purpose.

"These islands, son, guard the land like Fort Sumter guarded Charleston Harbor. Nothing comes up these creeks without passing the spirit gauntlet the Seewee built, their buried amulets and sacrifices—canine or human or whatever—still doing their duty though the priests are long gone and the gods they served uncalled on. But now, now that the professors have looted the Seewees' sacred sites, God only knows what's swimming landward, with nothing to stop it."

So much bullshit, you think, and so did I, safe in the Shenandoah, five hundred miles between me and the Seewee's empty shrines. Then I walked home one night from Sarah's. We were still courting; I lived in town and she lived eight miles out. It was summer, I'd had just enough wine to think an eight-mile-hike at midnight reasonable, and so I went, entranced by the stars and the warm night air and the roadside glowworms. The wine wore off and, night being night, footsteps died when I halted to hear them better, rustling leaves grew silent when I'd glance in their direction, and inexplicably cold pockets of air floated round me as I walked up Toad Run. Then I heard what I hadn't heard in thirty-five years—cre-e-ahh-haugh, cre-e-ahh-haugh, cre-e-ahh-haugh—and the whoosh of wings in the night.

20

The Goat Man

Goat Island lies beneath the new high rise bridge to the Isle of Palms. Chock-a-block with houses and docks, it butts up to a dredge spoil island four times its size. The owners are proud that you must still take a boat to get to "their" island.

A couple named the Holloways once called Goat Island home. He had been a butcher by trade, selling meats from a stall in the Charleston Market, a place where today you can buy a made-in-elsewhere Charleston souvenir and rub shoulders with people from everywhere but Charleston. He and his wife lived on the Neck, a narrow portion of the Charleston peninsula now given over to industry and cemeteries. They fled the city when interfering neighbors decided to lock her up for being crazy.

She had "fits," Daddy said, though no one now knows what caused these fits, whether menopause or epilepsy or anger or alcohol or angst. Even now, your neighbors, if they think you're a danger to them or yourself, can get you locked up on the word of a doctor or two. It's hell to pay to get out. I once helped a fellow student voluntarily commit himself. You're supposed to get out after forty-eight hours if you want out. That's what they told us as we signed my friend in for what we thought was a weekend, and he walked through a door the white clad staff locked after him. It took nearly a month, however, and lawyers, and a trip to court to spring him; the state is loathe to free those it thinks it should help.

So I know what busy-bodying neighbors can accomplish when they set their shallow, antiseptic souls to searing others. The Holloways must have surmised as much and wisely fled to the Isle of Palms, which was mostly undeveloped then. They hid out near a spring, built a log cabin from palmettos, and started what would be their forty-year hermitage. They lived off the creek and their herd of goats, traded oysters for supplies and week-old newspapers at a bait shop on the next island down, raided tomato fields on the mainland, cadged food from yachts on the Intracoastal Waterway, and feasted on turtle eggs, mullet, shrimp, crab and oyster. The Great Depression passed them by, as did World War II, the Atomic Age, the Cold War, Ike, Ozzie and Harriet, McCarthyism, and Sputnik.

Then development found them. A rich man bought the island, had it laid out in lots. His men found the Holloways who, unknown to themselves, had squatters' rights by this time. The developer knew, though, and had them run out. They fled across the Waterway to an unnamed island, what we now call Goat Island, a patch of sand so near sea-level nothing but palmettos can grow on it. They salvaged what they could, which wasn't much, and rounded up as many goats as they could. Winter was coming on, and they built themselves a cave in the side of a sand dune, and kept it from falling in on them by wedging whatever wood floated up on their island. When it got cold, they brought the goats inside a brush enclosure; when it got real cold, they brought them into the cave with them.

That's when people started calling him the Goat Man. You didn't want to get downwind of him when you met him—or between him and his wife. He took to carrying a shotgun with him, and he'd wave it around if you came too close to her. Naturally, he was meaner than ever, but he never bothered anybody until they decided to put houses on Goat Island.

That's when I met the Goat Man and Goat Lady. Daddy had gotten to know them over the years, and had written several articles for the paper on them. He visited them from time to time, after a hard winter or hurricane, to see how they were. He took me with him one time. I remember a wild-looking John-Brown-gone-to-seed sort of man, tall and skinny with long hair and a longer beard, and a shotgun. The shotgun was battered and beaten and so rusty, Daddy told me, it'd probably blow up in Holloway's face if he tried firing it. Mrs. Holloway hung in the background, a large woman in a faded and tattered dress. Both were dark as swamp water, stank to high hell, looked ferocious, and were absolutely charming to a scared young boy clinging to his father's pants leg. Holloway showed me the jewels of his beach combing—a whale's vertebra larger than my head yet light enough for a boy to lift with one hand; weird woods twisted to phantasmagoric shapes—snakes and elephants and giraffes; pieces of ships sunk in the sea; fragments of shrimp nets; bones of sea and land creatures; and shells of every description imaginable.

They're long gone now. Some say Mr. Holloway got so protective of his wife once people started building on Goat Island that he became dangerous; that both of them were getting old; that there wasn't room enough for their goats and all the houses. It was Mrs. Holloway, they say, who did it, somehow got hold of the authorities and had both of them carted off to an old folks home miles from the sea. There they died, anonymous and unknown, two old curmudgeons no one ever visited.

They left more traces of their presence here than most of us ever will. Big Goat and Little Goat islands are now official places on the map. There are still feral goats on the smaller islands no one wants to develop and the dredge spoil islands no one can develop. There are still my memories of them: Holloway visits occasionally, showing up when I least want and most need to see him, when my soul's suffocating, when I've almost convinced myself that this is the best of all possible worlds, that there really isn't any frontier left, that there's no way left to be free in America, that I'm doing the best I can, that God understands. Then Holloway appears, standing beside his driftwood fence, his cave and his goats and his wife, together forever, for richer, for poorer, for better, for worse, in sickness and in health, forsaking all others, and keeping only unto themselves, till death did them part.

They are the only truly free people I have ever met. Hallowed be their names.

21

Bull Island

From Porcher's Bluff, we used to look out nights on primordial darkness. Nothing lay between us and the ocean but the uninhabited end of the Isle of Palms and Dewee's and Caper's and Bull islands. We knew the islands were there, three miles out, but at night they vanished in the dark. When the stars came up, and the wind blew the sound of the surf inland, we could almost believe that what we saw was what the Seewee had seen before our people dispossessed them.

First came the Army Corps of Engineers' green channel marker which hung in the night like the light that beckoned Gatsby from the end of Daisy's dock. Only what it beckoned were developers. Now the Isle of Palms and Dewee's Island lie upon the night horizon like becalmed and garish ocean liners. Where once the Goat Man wandered, lovers strolled, and camping children pretended to be castaways, now rise hotels and cheek-by-jowl row houses, a marina and golf course, all vying for who can project the most and brightest lights. Dewee's, a deserted haven all my life until now, has sprouted its own luminescent fungi. Enterprising developers have floated bulldozers and dump trucks and cranes, and all the paraphernalia necessary to building beach houses, to an island so exclusive you have to take a boat to get to it. Where stars rose five years ago shine amber-colored high-vapor and white house lights, illuminating million dollar dreams made real. Daytime visits discover "No Trespassing" signs staked on the front row of dunes where once turtles crawled and I sprawled. Bulldozers scrape the beach to protect brand new houses from erosion.

To reach Dewee's, nearest of these barrier islands, is an hour-and-a-half canoe ride down Porcher's twists and turns to Shark Hole's daunting depths, a quick dash across the Waterway in the wake of passing barges or yachts and, fighting the sea swell in the inlet, beaching myself before the current can carry me beyond Dewee's, and into the sea itself.

Sharing an island with bulldozers is little fun, and so Sarah and I decided to visit Bull Island, two islands farther up the coast. "You'll never find your way through Copahee," my father said the first time we proposed the trip. "I know only one other man who ever knew the way through, and he's dead. And what the hell do you want to take a woman, much less your wife, out there in a canoe for anyway?" Daddy is given to over-estimating the difficulty of tasks his children set themselves to—Copahee is hardly the obstacle he paints it to be—but everyone is hero of his own dreams, Freud claimed, and who am I to begrudge my father, hero of this narrative, his embellishing his forays into the marsh?

A midday high tide is perfect for visiting Bull Island—three hours out with the ebb tide, three hours beachcombing, and three hours back on flood tide, providing luck and the wind hold. To navigate the shoals that separate Porcher's from Copahee requires a nearly full tide; within an hour after the tide turns, oysters break the surface, barring passage. Halfway across Copahee, miles from land, I've run aground on oyster banks. Like a young Sam Clemens on the Mississippi, I had to learn to read the water, looking for telltale darker water marking shallow reefs, and riffles and ripples that, ignoring the wind, marked underwater shoals. Sunlight glints off chop thrown up by the tide, fighting the wind until the sound becomes a fractured mirror reflecting a thousand different suns. The currents twist this way and that across the open sheet of water, following meanders secret at high tide.

At low tide, they lie bare to the passing world, which is pelicans and porpoises and Sarah and myself. Few humans venture into Copahee's shoal waters at low tide. In my youth I could lose myself in their maze for hours at a time, confident that the worst that could happen was sunburn as I waited for the rising tide to lift me higher than the oyster hedges flanking me.

In the meantime, I would explore a dozen islands buried at high tide, christening them Baffin and Guinea and Zealand and Hawaii and all the other names of islands I had—and have—never visited but in the mind. Like a Columbus, I stepped ashore an undiscovered isle, but upon me the native oysters spat, armies of pistol shrimp fired, and toadfish grinned from armored bunkers.

My father and I used to sit side by side on an oyster bank and dine on oysters only seconds out of the water. At such times, oysters seem to be creek concentrate, shell-bound distillations of the sea itself. They slide down, more liquid than flesh, the same temperature, the same salinity, as the ambient water. We'd pass each other the gallon water jug whose rim tasted of salt and mud but whose contents were pure delight after two hours in the salt. So too Sarah and I sat on upturned buckets on a nameless oyster bank and dined on oysters on the half shell that quivered when we squirted lemon on them. We rinsed our mouths of Copahee's salt with white wine, and almost called the trip off, so content did we feel.

The call of Bull Island could not be denied; before we saw the sea, we heard and felt it. The dull rush of the surf had sung to us throughout the voyage, blown in by a headwind. Nearing the end of the island just south of Bull we felt, faint and feeble, the pulse of the sea swell as it lifted and dropped our canoe. It built, and soon the canoe was rising and falling as we headed straight into the swell, its crest fretted with foam that blew across our gunwales. We were caught in the current, though, and no wind or sea swell could stop us now, as we and all of the water pooled three miles wide and ten miles long behind the islands rushed out through the inlet.

I grew up on my father's tales of Bull Island. From his home at Walnut Grove on the mainland, he could see the island's tree line. Like me, he dreamed dreams based on his father's tales of its white sands and black lagoons, its fifteen-foot alligators and sea-going turtles. Unlike me, he went there with his father.

"Bull's Bay was my stomping ground," he used to say. "I knew every shoal and bar and bank from Alligator Creek to Jack's Creek, from Up and Down Creek to Oyster Bay. I hunted Bull Island so many times I could take you up Summerhouse Creek blindfolded. Your mother and I spent our honeymoon there, back when they still had an inn on the island. Goddamn government closed it down years ago."

Summers we went to Bull's Bay where he taught me how to throw a cast net, to reach into burrows after stone crabs, to feel out clams with my feet. We visited the Bay's pelican and tern rookeries, watched for loggerhead turtles on Cape Island and horseshoe crabs in its marshes. Bull Island, a green line on the horizon, was always "next time"; like Virginia Woolf's lighthouse, though, "next time" never came.

That is, until Sarah and I canoed over. Where my father had walked as a boy was now a mile out to sea. Where he and my mother had lain nude on a deserted beach was sunk under ten feet of salty water—so fast are his past and the island eroding. The Bull Island he and mother enjoyed was one of sandy lanes, shaded by one-hundred-fifty-year-old pines growing out of a savannah of grass in which the sea breeze traced whimsical patterns and kept the mosquitoes down. Bull Island was ground zero in 1989 for Hurricane Hugo, whose one-hundred-forty mile-an-hour winds blew a twenty-foot wall of water over the ten-foot-high island, snapping off nearly every pine tree twenty feet above ground, ripping the leaves and moss off live oaks, and shredding the palmettos' fronds. Today the salt-blanched, barkless grey trunks of shattered pines rise out of a jungle of scrub and poison ivy that blocks the breeze and harbors hordes of mosquitoes. Live oaks lift still-ravaged limbs heavenward, and hundreds of palmettos have yet to grow back their fronds.

Though bedraggled, the island is still magnificent. Sarah, who has swam in the South and North Pacifics, the China and Japan seas, the Indian Ocean and the Mediterranean Sea, the Irish and North seas, the English Channel, the Atlantic Ocean and the Caribbean Sea, who has sat by fires on Tahitian beaches, watched the Southern Cross rise over Bora Bora, tickled giant clams on Australia's Great Barrier Reef, roasted fish under coconut palms in Malaysia, eaten sushi beside the Inland Sea, and watched the sun rise or set on a hundred different beaches in nearly as many lands, says that Bull Island is "the most beautiful beach in the world."

To see it, we walked two miles through a live oak and palmetto maritime forest which ended abruptly at the beach's edge. The beach lay littered with the drowned remains of former forest. Palmettos leaned and arced and toppled along the forest edge, and the trunks of those already dead lay marooned in sand, their frond-and-root-stripped trunks so many fallen phalluses of a defunct religion. Live oaks reached tortured, arthritic limbs heavenward like the hands of aged devotees, imploring a deaf and heedless ocean to cease its gnawing.

One could not have imagined this beach. From the sea, the trees marched landward, their water-washed grey and leafless trunks giving way to sparsely-leafed trees supplanted by forests of green as if this were evolution's beachhead.

Between the grey and brown trunks, the sand was blindingly white. Farther down, beyond the forest, the sand stretched seaward through a shallow gully warmed to bathtub temperature, then rose and shelved off into the ocean. This far from any river, the water was blue, nearly transparent, and the surf gentle, soothing. Beyond the surf, nothing for four thousand miles but ocean.

The beach was deserted save for us. No footprints preceded us, no refuse from passing fishermen. I was Milton's Adam and Sarah his Eve, "the world was all before us . . . hand in hand, with wandering step and slow, through Eden we took our solitary way."

My oldest sister, who has never visited Bull Island, thinks she was conceived there, and the dates corroborate her supposition. Let us suppose a family tradition and say that our son Edward was also conceived on this edge of the continent, on the remnants of the beach upon which my parents began their marriage, and upon which the first English settlers landed. It was here, not Charleston, that they made landfall and were greeted by Indians clad, like I clad Sarah, in naught but Spanish moss.

Spanish moss with red bugs; if Bull Island is Eden, it is an Eden after the fall. Snakes slither through its undergrowth and sun on its paths, leaving their serpentine trails as warnings of their presence. Turkeys lurk in the shade of oaks, and burst skyward in explosions of gobbles and flapping feathers and shaking branches that left me shaking even worse. Their tracks resemble nothing so much as dinosaur prints, three toes to the front and one to the rear, the track of a three-foot-tall bird that might, on this island, be instead the trail of a saurian raptor enamoured of mammal meat.

Bull Island seems a relic of a pre-mammalian era, a hundred–million-year-old fragment from the Age of Reptiles. Twenty-four different kinds of reptile share these woods: snakes, turtles and alligators, everywhere alligators. Their crawls crisscrossed our trail across a narrow dike; clawed footprints larger than my outspread hand flanked the trace of tails dragged through the sand like impossibly enlarged versions of lizard tracks. Fish scales from that morning's breakfast littered the bank. Five-foot alligators floated in the tea-dark water of trailside creeks. On the far bank, a twelve-foot behemoth sunned under a palmetto tree. Crossing a dike, we heard the plop-plop of a dozen sixteen-inch yellow-black yearling gators scuttling into the water, sinking and rising again, floating legs akimbo in miniature versions of their ten-times-longer mother—whom we discovered grinning in the water five feet behind us. She was blessedly lethargic in the cool air of March; three months later when we returned, she and her kind were frighteningly quick, spinning round on their tails and lashing out with a hiss when disturbed, sliding into the water with a slap that splattered us with duckweed and muck.

The dike we stood on dammed the upper reaches of Jack's Creek, a forty-foot-deep creek with plenty of fresh water known to the early Spanish explorers who sheltered in its mouth behind Bull Island's hook-shaped northern end. "You know damn well they buried doubloons out there," Daddy would bellow. "Of course, they're three fathoms down now, thanks to the god-damned Army Corps of Engineers' misbegotten flood projects." The English diked the creek, impounding the marsh to grow rice, and built against Spanish and French raiders and pirates of all nationalities a fort whose tabby ruins still stand in the woods. Smugglers still sail these waters, and the local paper announces from time to time a Bull Island drug bust or corpse.

Before Europeans there were Indians whose middens line the inland marsh side of Bull Island, remnants of centuries of feasting on oysters. Judging from their pottery designs, these were the same people as those who dined along Porcher's Creek.

Not that we stole any shards; Bull Island today is part of the Cape Romain National Wildlife Refuge, ninety thousand acres forever protected from development. The only way there is by water, and the beach is a two-mile walk from the dock. The government forbids overnight visits.

There was nothing for it but to paddle back. Sunburned, sore and tired, we began our journey home, retracing our morning path. This time we had the wind and tide with us, and we rigged our beach umbrella in the bow like a spinnaker and fairly clipped along on the straight stretches, Sarah hanging perilously out to peer around the umbrella, shouting "oysters to starboard," "mudbank to port," "fishermen dead ahead." We wound our way homeward through marsh and sound; feeding porpoise rose to greet us with their fixed smiles, wetting our faces with their windblown spouts, miniature versions of Moby Dick, of whom their pale blue, almost white skins, scarred and streaked with cuts and scratches, reminded us. They sounded and were gone, replaced by elegant black and red and white skimmers who sliced the water like can openers in search of fish. Oyster catchers screeched at our ungainly silhouette from the banks where they were busy searching out supper. A convoy of heavily laden pelicans glided before us, seventeen in a militarily precise formation, escorting us across Copahee, and into the setting sun and Porcher's before banking left and seaward.

Dehydrated, exhausted, our very eyeballs sunburned, but ecstatic over our trip, we struggled up the dock, and onto land, and into reality.

My father was ensconced, as usual, in his chair, listening to Rush Limbaugh's version of reality. "Well, you finally got back. Catch anything for supper?" he asked.

22

Triage

September is harvest month in the marsh, and the heads of *Spartina* lie heavy and bent with seed. To row through the marsh now is to pass through a golden shower before, behind, above, between, below. Everywhere saucy grasshoppers leapfrog from stem to stem like troops of primates, sprinkling the water with gold whenever they land upon a ripened head of seed. Grasshoppers, careless and carefree as the fading summer, green and brown like the marsh they eat, are food themselves for pale spiders, nearly invisible in their hideaways between grass blade and stem. When the wind is from the west, thousands of these spiders' distant cousins float through the sky, borne up on strands of silk they spin out and out until the wind catches them and they're off to worlds unknown and, over Porcher's, inevitable death by drowning. An incessant whining like mosquitoes in the lee of the boat betrays a thousand marsh midges blackening gunwale and hull, hanging like living beards, shifting this way and that as the wind plays at their convocation's edges.

Higher and higher the tide rises until the very tops of the marsh are nearly buried and, like invisible ink made visible, slow eddies reveal their presence in pools and puddles of seed. Even the most inaccessible reaches of the marsh yield up their secrets. Out of an abandoned marsh wren's woven softball of a nest peers a mouse; evicted by the rising tide, he swims to a nearby half-finished nest that in its day served as a decoy to predators, and now serves one as a refuge. White, conical snails shaped like lopsided Hershey's Kisses ride the tops of marsh stems to escape the two-to-four-foot-long spot-tailed bass hunting the water below. Carolina's own escargot, these periwinkles once fed

Indians, and their presence in a shell-heap is a sure sign that it's Indian. No one but the curious or hard-hearted eat them now, since fifty must die to furnish an appetizer.

Come autumn, when the tides were especially high, we went marsh hen hunting. Normally, we never saw marsh hens. Secretive birds the size of starved chickens, they sidle through and between the marsh, hiding in its green shadows, but we heard them everywhere. One delivers its raucous, wild cackle, and the marsh responds, everywhere, indignant and invisible hens cackling their outrage at the shadow of a raptor or cloud or God himself.

Autumnal tides, driven higher and higher by the mysteries of the equinox, flooded the marsh, licking at the land in a biennial anticipation of the time when all this would be fathoms deep. Just as the rising water drove grasshopper and spider and periwinkle farther and farther up their precarious marsh refuges until, top-heavy with the weight of the marooned, the marsh bent and delivered its burden of life to the jaws of waiting fish, so the tide drove marsh hens out of their customary haunts. They floated with the marsh wrack and hid themselves amid a crowd of golden seed.

The night before marsh henning I spent cleaning my father's father's shotgun, running an oil-soaked rag in and out of the bore until not a particle of dust or powder disturbed its sheen. My father's "that'll do" was all the praise I needed. Surrounded by the smell of gun and oil and old canvas and leather, lost in boyish fantasies of what I imagined manhood to be, I undid the cardboard box of brass-ended shotgun shells, held their hard, red shapes to my nose, and sniffed like a connoisseur of Havannas before loading our jackets' pockets with them.

Duck hunters suffer through winter dawns and pouring rain, but the gods smile on marsh hen hunters, sending us late morning high tides, blue skies and mild, sweater weather. Daddy and I would drive down to the marsh, pull the bateau out from where we'd stowed it for the winter under the dock's sheltering boardwalk, right it, load poles and thermos and canvas jackets heavy with shells, and push the boat to the water's edge. When I had seated myself in the bow, Daddy would break down the shotgun, checking that it was, indeed, empty, and hand it to me. "Here, you take this, boy, and keep it dry," he'd say, pushing us out into the marsh and jumping into the stern, rocking us with his weight. Then he'd take the hickory sapling his father had fashioned years before into a pole and push us into the creek. Once there, the flood tide bore us far into the marsh, up grasping fingers of creek narrower than my childhood waist and out and over creekbanks into the heavy-headed marsh itself, until it seemed we'd punted all the way to Iowa on amber waves of salt marsh.

When the last houses had sunk behind the silhouette of marsh and island, Daddy would have me load the shotgun. I'd cradle it between my knees, its barrel pointed high enough to keep out water and seed, my left hand on its safety, and follow the rhythm of my father's poling, rocking backwards as the bateau slid from under me each time my father dug into the mud and pushed us forward, then sailing through the marsh in equilibrium, loose and free until the grass itself slowed the bateau, and I felt myself sliding forward off my seat, yanked back at the very edge by my father's next push forward. Settling into a silent routine, we waited the frantic skyward burst from under our bow as a hen, homeless and landless, took to the air in low, fast flight, cackling in fright and anger, the entire marsh resounding with a chorus of indignant kin. I'd raise the barrel, follow, catch and lead the frantic feathers and, flicking off the safety and pulling every so slightly back upon the trigger with my left forefinger, in an explosion louder and harsher than anything alive can make, blow hen to death and marsh to silence.

In the shocked silence that followed, my ears rang, gun shoulder ached, nostrils flared and tongue watered with the mingled smell and taste of gunpowder. Perhaps like us, God too ponders in the silence that follows his catastrophes: was it worth it? Did he, she, it, they have to die? Life would reassert, then, itself in a flurry of noise and activity. "Over there, about a hundred feet to port." "I see her, just beyond that wrack." "Yeah, yeah, I'll get her." We'd pole toward an island of dead and floating marsh grass, beyond which lay the mangled corpse of what we would eat that night.

A plucked and gutted marsh hen looks like a gangly Cornish game hen or a starved and dwarfish chicken, only brown, and a dozen times more flavorful. Muscled and lean and gamey, every bite reminding me of the marsh and the hunt and, yes, that this meat I chew was once, like me, alive, that I murder to eat. Better far for my soul that I know this, acknowledge the unrinsable blood staining my hands, than that I pretend the bland mound of meat that is a store-bought chicken did not die for my gluttony.

Marsh hens seldom let me forget the pain of their deaths, often as not falling only wounded into the flooded marsh. Then it was we poled towards a small commotion, a barely noticeable rippling in the grass a hundred feet away. Our bateau parted the marsh grass, moving like a predator itself, sniffing out the dying. The conversation repeated itself: "Over there, about a hundred feet to port," "I see her, just beyond that wrack." "Yeah, yeah, I'll get her." I'd lean over as the boat slid by and grab the struggling bird around her torso, lift her, and wring her neck.

I remember my first such moment, the wounded bird fluttering in frantic agony, her faint and feeble efforts at flight when lifted up out of the water. Cradling her in one hand, I reached for her neck, impossibly long, feathers and skin ripped by my pellets' passage to reveal reddish brown sinews and blue and red blood vessels, her head hanging at a sick angle from off her wreck of a neck. I wrung and wrung her neck in gruesome mockery of a cartoon character's corkscrewed neck, to no avail. "I can't kill her, Daddy. She won't die." He reached forward, took the bird that I had first wounded, then tortured. Holding her round her chest, he beat her head again and again against the gunwale. "There, son," he said, handing her back, dead. "Always know how to kill what you wound."

Once my family had been out driving, my father at the wheel. He rounded the corner and there, in the middle of the road, stood a hound. Too close to avoid, too close to do anything but hit. A thud and then a howl of pain when our two thousand pounds of car travelling at fifty-miles-per-hour struck flesh and bone. Daddy pulled over to the side, told us to stay in the car, and got out. He opened the trunk, rummaged around, took out the lug wrench and walked back to where the dog lay writhing on the asphalt. He knelt down on one knee, head bent, in similar pose, I remember thinking, to George Washington all those Valley Forge portraits hanging in our schools. He raised the wrench and brought it down three times on the dog's head. Daddy rose and carried wrench and dog to the road's edge, dropped the dog in the weeds, wiped the lug wrench off in grass, came back, put it back in the trunk, opened the door, climbed in and sat there for a moment before starting the engine. A long moment for his children. He looked around at us, catching each of us in the eye, and said, "Always kill what you wound."

Once, walking through Porcher's woods, I scared up an egret. A beautiful thing, wings spread, neck bent in a perfect S of a curve, legs outstretched, it rose from the forest floor towards the sky, and hit a pine branch, crumpled and fell not twenty feet from me. It struggled on the ground, wing broken, its feathers spread and erect, as beautiful in its fright as a mating egret is in its dance. Egret and human stared at each other, and it waited, as if we were both caught up in a proscribed ritual. I, priest; egret, sacrifice; my sacrifice blessing me with its steady gaze, and waiting for me to bash it to death. Apostate, I fled, dodging tree trunks and branches, brambles gripping me, tripping me, myrtle tearing at my face, pines ripping my clothes as they vainly tried to grab me, to hold me, to return me to my duty, to force me to kill what I had wounded.

I did not, could not, would not. That egret and marsh hen haunt me more than all the birds and rabbits and squirrel I have killed, more than all the chickens and pigs and cattle others have butchered for me to eat, more than all the fish and shrimp and crabs and clams and oysters I have suffocated and eaten. Strange that I'd feel better if, instead of giving up, instead of fleeing, I had wrung a neck and beat a feathered skull to a bloody pulp.

There are wounds worse than the physical, self-inflicted, like those I gouged into my soul when I abandoned my responsibility to two dumb brutes. Those that I have gouged into mine own and others' hearts and souls. No doubt we all have our private list of those we are ashamed to face, people we have somehow hurt beyond repair or forgiveness by design or accident, and who we have not yet had the courage to kill, to lay to rest by forgetting or by asking for forgiveness, for benediction. Orestes all, we are pursued by Furies of our own invention, demons we have made of others we are now too scared or embarrassed to beg intercession of. None of us is without sin, and yet it is we sinners who must cast the stones, raise the lug wrenches, shoulder the guns, the sticks, the branches, the telephones or pen and paper, and beat those that we have crippled and wounded. Else they live forever, reversing roles, haunting and hounding and hunting us until we learn by bitter experience to kill what we wound.

23

The Princess

Once upon a long, long time ago, my father danced with a princess.

One day he took us to her place. We headed far up river, and kept going on and on, farther than we were used to going, to the verge of terra incognito, to beyond where there be dragons. We were packed into the bateau, putt-putting upstream, the river licking our bow and drooling a bit onto our floorboards at the prospect of our capsize. He took us under a drawbridge rusted shut in disuse; past fossil beds drowned beneath six feet of water; past Indian Point, its oyster middens winking whitely at us, promising pottery should we stop; past marsh hummocks crowned with cedar and palmetto in whose green thickets hid rusting fifty gallon drums and coiled metal tubes, Prohibition's jetsam; past shrimp hole and mullet hole; and on and on into stretches which had no landmarks for us children, but which our father knew from forty years before.

Then a right turn into a wide-mouthed creek whose sinuous turns enticed us ever onward, through hectares of marsh pathless save for the creek. Daddy summoned up for us browsing deer, and sliding otters, and snowy egrets that burst whitely into the sky at our approach, their yellow-slippered feet peeping out from a froth of plumes. On the branch of an overhanging live oak sat an orange-colored marsh coon regarding us like some Lowcountry version of the Chesire Cat. Bend after bend we followed the creek inland, swinging to port and then to starboard with each ox-bowed meander. Then, rounding a point, we had arrived, as Daddy had promised, at the princess's.

Ancient live oaks shaded a grassy bluff whose retaining wall had tumbled here and there in disarray. Quarried stone the size of shoe boxes paved the intertidal reaches of the bank, marsh grass growing between and fiddlers playing king of the mountain atop every block. "Belgian blocks," our father called them, cutting the motor. We conjured visions of Europe, tall gabled houses flanking a plaza whose seaward side was lined with ships up whose gangplanks stevedores pushed sideless wheelbarrows stacked with these grey ingots called Belgian blocks. "An Italian princess had them brought in by boat. Once all this land was hers. She'd arrive by river; the state built the drawbridge downriver especially for her."

"I came here first when I was a teenager," he continued, letting us drift landward, the ebbing tide slowing us so that we came ashore gently, almost reverently. "Back then, the house still stood, and all of this was lawn and garden."

Daddy took us ashore and pointed through the gloom of live oaks. "The house was there," he said. Framed by the trees a wall rose four stories into the forest canopy. Tendrils of wisteria clambered through the vacant windows, throwing us welcoming bouquets of flowers as we climbed a shattered and leaf-strewn staircase to what had been, in my father's youth, the front door. We stood ten feet above the forest floor, and fireplaces stood hearthless and mantleless ten and twenty feet above us. Below us, the leaf litter parted here and there, revealing teasing fragments of a tiled floor.

"We danced over there," my father said, pointing to an airy nothingness to our left. "The ballroom ran the length of the house, took up nearly half the first floor. Its walls were cypress panels three hundred years old; chairs and settees that had cushioned Revolutionaries and Redcoats in one war and Confederates in another lined the walls. Flowers were everywhere. Down that end, on a raised stage, she had a string orchestra. The windows were open and, when the orchestra was silent, you could hear the tree frogs."

We children ran down the stairs out into what had been gardens. Giant camellias still framed forgotten alleys that tunneled towards infinity through a green gloom lit with the ruby glow of azaleas. A bevy of gardenias bloomed white and pale in what must have been a private garden off an alley, and the air was heavy with their thick, sweet odor. We discovered a swimming pool slowly filling with duckweed and cattails, its broken diving board become a turtles' sunning spot. Serpentine walls only a brick thick snuck hither and yon through the shade.

We passed an afternoon in this forgotten world, returning to the landing when summoned by our father, who had spent the time with his dreams. We ate our sandwiches propped up against the roots of the oaks, cushioning ourselves with pillows of Spanish moss that hung in ropes from every branch. "My parents had brought me along thinking it might be fun for me," Daddy said, taking up where he'd left off. "I was in my uncle's tuxedo, feeling overdressed and out of place, conspicuous and inconspicuous at the same time. Of course, I hadn't danced all night, not knowing anyone, you see. Not that I'd really minded; I'd spent the time watching the others, beautiful women bare-shouldered and evening-gowned, their jewelry sparkling in the candlelight. The room was lit by candles in hurricane glasses all along the walls and two massive chandeliers you could lower by chain to replenish. The couples whirled in and out of shadow and light, around and around and around one another, first the women like magnificent birds, and then their escorts in black, then the women again, then their escorts, and so on and on through the night. In the middle of them all danced the princess and her husband, the rich American who'd bought her this place. The music stopped when they were just in front of me, and they both came over to where I stood, and she said to me in a voice as beautiful as I had dreamt it must be, "Would you dance this one with me?" Tripping over my feet and my tongue, I did, and I danced my first and last with a princess. Then the music ended and I became a pumpkin."

We left soon after that in the growing dark. Daddy rowed us downcreek so as not to break the spell he and her house had woven round us. "It burned not long after," he explained in a voice as quiet as the world had become, "in a fire that lit these woods up more than any of her parties ever did. Some say it was a disgruntled worker, some say it was electrical." He rowed a bit and said, "She left by river and never returned. The bridge they built especially for her has not opened since."

We all looked back at the ruins before they disappeared around a bend. The fireflies had come out, lighting up her empty windows from time to time like candles from my father's far away youth. Then her house was gone. Daddy cranked up the motor and we returned to the mainstream, and home.

I'd journey back to the princess's on my own from time to time, and spend a lazy afternoon wandering her fading garden and gazing up at her empty windows, cutting in on my father's memory, and dancing in my daydreams with a princess I'd never meet. Then loggers bought the land from whoever owned it, bulldozing tracks through her garden and razing her camellias. Developers finished the job, filling in her swimming pool and tearing down what was left of her house. What had been a plantation they subdivided and sold off as tiny lots—so small "you can look into your neighbor's bathroom and watch him brush his teeth," as my father put it—a "gated community" in which we are not welcome.

24

Sex

As I got older, mating crabs provided me peculiarly inappropriate lessons in sex education. Blue crabs are easy to sex; the males' apron is long and slender, the females' shorter and thicker. Upon attaining sexual maturity, immature females' triangular aprons grow to resemble, as one guidebook says, the outline of the Capitol Building in Washington. My older sisters were undergoing a similar, albeit mammalian, version of sexual maturation, and in the creek alone with me my father explained what was happening to them by reference to "girl crabs." "Your sisters are coming into their prime and changing their shapes, just like a girl crab'll do," he'd say, and we'd have an impromptu anatomy lesson with whatever crabs we'd happened to catch. When we found a mating pair, my father, mixing metaphors and species, explained, "One of these days, you're going to start sniffing girls just like a hound does a bitch. And then you're going to want to do what these boys are doing, get yourself a girl, cuddle up to her, and make yourself a mess of baby crabs." He'd peel back the male's apron and show me the crab's "two penises" running either underside of the apron. I misunderstood this crab and dog version of the birds and the bees, and I anticipated growing a second penis, which would have the added benefit of proving that men did not make babies by peeing on women, as I had vaguely thought they had before.

No more powerful aphrodisiac exists than the creek, whose funky smells are sex's grand originals. Porcher's waters are a stew of the sperm, smelt, jism, eggs, roe, sprat and fry of countless species, its mingled salts and mud and rot a perfume more powerful than any Parisian imitation. Her waters, salt and fresh, were a voyeur's paradise. Besides the usual array of copulating cattle, fornicating dogs, and humping horses, I watched while crabs lay in amorous embrace for hours; male damselflies grabbed their female counterparts by the neck and forced them hither and yon, alighting on my shoulders in post coital exhaustion; male dragonflies fought noisy clashes of brittle wings for the rights to twenty feet of muscle beach creekbank from which to woo passing females; enormous female grasshoppers quietly chewed their dinner and two or three males jostled each other for a place upon their abdomens while I, acutely aware of my left-handed minority status, waited to see whether they wrapped their own abdomens left to right or right to left around their paramours; herons courted each other deep in the swamps in stylized and awkward dances as beautiful and exotic as an Oriental mime; lovebugs flew and ate locked in perpetual embrace; butterflies spiraled heavenward in mutual seduction; male seagulls choked their nesting loves with gifts of fish; aphids gave virgin birth to pregnant daughters; in the clear reaches of fresh water, male fish fought for muddy nests and minnows turned bright colors and huddled and humped in groups; midges and gnats danced up and down in aerial sex shows; and female fiddlers strutted their wares before a thousand flushed and fiddling males. The very flowers were sexual organs open to any passing bee or bug or hummingbird.

Few girlfriends actually enjoyed the creek as I did. I kept trying, revealing my secret world to girls I especially liked the way more fashionable boys might have taken their dates to a movie or nightclub. Between the mud and mosquitoes and horseflies and heat, few came back a second time. Those that did, I treated to a world as new and wonderful to them as the world of sex was to us both. One day we lay like blue crabs embraced and unmoving for so long on a sand flat that the buzzards swooped down to examine us; another we became sunburned watching fiddlers; another we imitated herons stalking minnows, swooped like skimmers through the water, and plunged like pelicans into mullet holes. Where before I had worked myself and the marsh, judging a day a loss if I returned with an empty bucket, I now seldom returned with anything but an empty bucket and a full heart, and the joy of being close to another human being. Casting a net was an excuse for closeness, mud required held hands, deep water an embrace. We stripped each other's shrimp cooked over a driftwood fire on our own private island in the marsh, anticipated stripping each other of our clothes, and wondered whether the people who'd left the pottery and arrowheads we found at the feet of live oaks had cuddled as we did in their shade.

Those were heady days when we asked no more of each other than kisses lasting hours, and sex itself lay before us like the marsh at dawn, a new world waiting to explored. Now sex is like the marsh in late afternoon, well known and familiar, laden with memories pleasant and unpleasant. Over everything lies the trace of others who have shared with us these same pleasures. Kisses no longer suffice, no longer last for hours.

I am too familiar with myself as well, revisiting the same old trains of thought and memories and habits. My soul seems to me a giant rut, an entrenched creek bed grown as familiar as the road to work is for a commuter. With Wordsworth, I complain "That time is past, And all its aching joys are now no more,/ And all its dizzy raptures." Like he, "I have learned to look on nature, not as in the hour/ Of thoughtless youth; but hearing oftentimes/ The still, sad music of humanity."

Neither the marsh nor Sarah nor myself is virginal; we have all shared ourselves with others whose traces linger long after they have left. Like us, the marsh remembers others who have loved it and abused it—Indians whose islands yet remain, slaves whose ditchworks still work, farmers whose field rows sleep under pines, public-minded engineers whose DDT still lingers in the mud, Lelands whose footprints fill with mud, and suburbanites whose docks line Porcher's upper reaches. Like all lovers, I want to think I am that special someone, but who am I to say that the marsh prefers me to her other suitors? That my interests are her interests? Though I love Porcher's, I know she, like all nature, is indifferent. Whatever meaning I derive from her I have invented.

25

Faults

One hundred and sixty years ago, an earthquake shook this land. Rivers ran backwards, the earth split, and sand flowed like water. Five miles beneath us, so they say, where the pressure melts rock like ice, a fault line severs the very foundations of the earth. Back when the earth was all one continent and the oceans all one sea, America and Africa were one, joined right here, the joint as solid, as permanent as the land you walk today. Then the earth groaned and gave birth to the Atlantic Ocean. Those who know of such things say the land still bears the stretch marks of that birth, that here and there along this coast one can trace the ridges and troughs where the earth's skin stretched and buckled. Buried beneath the sandy foundations of my world snakes one such stretch mark, a sleeping fault whose nightmares send shudders through earth and humans, shaking our sandcastles. With so uncertain an earth to stand upon, who but a child could expect mere human foundations to be more solid?

Like everyone, I grew up thinking my family as solid as rock; the Lelands, a sort of human Gondwanaland. Eventually I learned that buried faults ran deep between us all, unsure sutures uniting husband and wife, parent and child, sibling and sibling. The Lelands were no more solid than the rock upon which Porcher's rests. Ever-widening rifts fragmented us, and what God had joined together, man dissevered. Like Gondwanaland's fragments, my family drifts through space and time dreaming of an irretrievable past. We have each gone walkabout in dream, in deep time, the time before time, the time before divorce, back when we all lived beside Porcher's.

Some say eels preserve similar memories, their fall migrations to the distant Sargasso Sea imposed by plate tectonics. Back when the newborn Atlantic was but a Red Sea, the eel began an instinctual journey that obligates each succeeding generation to make an ever-longer, ever-madder pilgrimage. Ornithologists suppose that tropic-wintering birds returning each summer to their temperate and Arctic nesting grounds follow an ancestral path not nearly so long two thousand generations ago, when tundra nesting grounds lay in southern Pennsylvania, and the boreal forests of Canada reached as far south as Porcher's Creek. Northward marching milkweeds drew in their van the monarch butterfly, which must flee the cold each fall, millions of monarchs riding the cold fronts south. As a child, I waded living rivers of orange in the lea of the sea island dunes until we reached land's end and, earthbound, yearned for I knew not what as the current spilled across the water and disappeared in the blue skies of the south.

Fractured, faulted, torn asunder, the Lelands drift, each member pulled towards his or her destiny by inscrutable, unreachable desires whose currents swirl us like butterflies in a wind, here throwing us together, there pulling us apart.

Exiled by divorce to town, my father made his backyard there a memorial to his lost gardens. Absconding from vacant woods with trunk load after trunk load of rich, black mold to spread over the rubble waste that was his backyard, planting strawberry and banana-scented trees, gardenias and oleanders, ginger lilies and sweet bay, lime and lemon trees, he fashioned a riot of perfumed beauty richer and ranker than that he'd left behind. Here, he could migrate to a time before rupture. It was his monument to memory, a bridge to span the many ruptures in a long life, his last attempt to scale the walls of Eden. For years he and his garden flourished, by slow degrees forgetting that freezes do come this far south; as one eventually did, leaving his banana grove drooping towards a putrid mush, his oleanders ashen grey, and his limes and lemons deciduous. Picking leaves stiff in death from his twelve-foot lemon tree, looking away and apropos of nothing and everything, he said to me, "You know, sometimes I wonder if it was worth it all."

Today, he once again lives beside Porcher's Creek, but not once in the twenty years since his divorce has he stepped into the creek he lost. Sweatered and hatted indoors though it be summer, he shivers in the sun and, drawing me with him, talks us back to other creeks and suns, wading Porchers of memory, drawn like the eels, the birds, the butterflies, by something in the blood that will not let us go.

Afterword

The old order changeth, yielding place to new,
And God fulfils himself in many ways,
Lest one good custom should corrupt the world.
Comfort thyself: what comfort is in me?

Alfred Lord Tennyson

We all remember a time when life was so perfect we could wish it might never end. For me, the first of these moments is walking a tidal creek with my father. Outlined by the rising sun, his cast net slung over his shoulder, lead weights swinging with every step, my father seems a god in silhouette. I follow with the bucket, watching the water fill his footsteps in the sand before me. We might have been walking like this forever; we might go on walking like this forever.

To think a mess of mullet could mean so much.

One September, my father laid his arm around my shoulder and we walked out to the edge of the creek we must leave, its shores having been sold by others to developers. In my other arm was my son, whom I let loose to play with cast off oyster shells and fleeing fiddler crabs. My father and I stood silent, regarding the creek he gave me when I was but a child, the creek into which he will never step again, and by which I will never live again, and which will be, if anything at all, but a summer stop to my son. The tide was ebbing, the oyster banks beginning to show, and the Indian islands' palmettos impossibly remote in the growing dark.

Up the creek, the lights of the new people came on. Out on the end of one dock, too far away to be heard, their movements like those of a muted television show, knelt a father and child, crabbing.

Strangers possess the land now; my family's time upon the creek has passed, my life and longing but a long farewell. Perhaps the last of the Seewees stood like we three stood that evening, regarding the future—my ancestors—dispossessing them like it dispossesses all who fail for whatever reasons to hold on to that which they love. I can but hope that crabbing child will grow to love the creek as I have, will walk her banks and fish her holes, commune with her past and hand her future to his children. May he, God willing, remember in some corner of his soul looking up from crabbing one evening to see three figures downstream disappearing in the dark.